Organization

Organization Smarts

Portable Skills for Professionals
Who Want to Get Ahead

David W. Brown

AMACOM

American Management Association
New York • Atlanta • Brussels • Buenos Aires • Chicago • London • Mexico City
San Francisco • Shanghai • Tokyo • Toronto • Washington, D.C.

This publication is designed to provide accurate and authoritative information in regard to the subject matter covered. It is sold with the understanding that the publisher is not engaged in rendering legal, accounting, or other professional service. If legal advice or other expert assistance is required, the services of a competent professional person should be sought.

Library of Congress Cataloging-in-Publication data has been applied for and is on record at the Library of Congress.

Printing number

10 9 8 7 6 5 4 3 2 1

CONTENTS

ACKNOWLEDGMENTS

The idea for this book came naturally from my earlier work with students at the Yale School of Management and my current work with students at the Milano Graduate School of Management and Urban Policy at New School University. Their talents and prospects are why I teach and why these pages contain so much of what I have learned from them as well as the practitioner experience that I have shared with them.

How do I acknowledge all the others that I have learned from? I can't, but their influence also informs each chapter of the book. I am especially grateful to friends and colleagues like Ed Koch, Bob Wagner, Jr., Judith Friedlaender, Art Swersey, Gary Brewer, Charles Lindblom, David Riesman, Parker Palmer, Mim Pride, Larry Cremin, David Mathews, Harry Boyte, Debi Witte, Bryna Sanger, and Ed Blakely.

And then there is my wife, Alice, who reads everything I write with a practiced classroom eye that improves whatever she finds. My son, Peter, and daughter, Sarah, hold me to their high standards too, and the love that we all share nourishes everything I do.

Organization
Smarts

INTRODUCTION

Moving On *and* Getting Ahead

"I always keep my résumé updated."
"Mine is on the Web all the time."

By choice or necessity, it's only natural to be restless in an era with new talent markets encouraging job and career mobility and so many organizations treating their employees like just-in-time inventory. From 1990 to 2000, the average employment tenure of American workers in any one organization was three years, and by 2000, it was only thirteen months in the high tech industry. During that decade, the number of those becoming "free agents" doubled to twenty-five million.[1]

This book is written for those who are always ready to move on, looking for a new challenge, a better deal, a chance to shine; quite simply, people who want to get ahead. Originally, finding a job was the goal. Then, it was getting an education that opened doors. Now, there is a restless and credentialed cohort with expectations for their working lives that no one organization is likely to satisfy. They are women who are not content with just bringing home a living wage or second income; they are professionals who see themselves entitled to the same autonomy and discretion that their professors enjoyed in graduate school; they are social entre-

1

preneurs who cross sectors looking to collaborate and combine resources; they are designers of software, carrying their assets in a laptop; and they are all the wannabes who consider life too short to wait for the promise of a gold watch. These are individual-centered prospectors, not organization-centered loyalists, looking for their own special gold that they have promised themselves and find worth pursuing from one organization to another.

People who change jobs frequently and those who are solo consultants know, however, that moving from one opportunity to another is not easy going. The personal advantage they seek for themselves can be offset by the disadvantage of working in unfamiliar organizations with relative strangers. What they learned at their last workplace does not have equal application in their new assignment. Every organization that they move on to is different from the last one, and they have to assess what those differences are and how to adapt to them. Unless they are entrepreneurs with their own start-ups or geniuses who don't need others as part of their gifted performance, they have a lot of adjustments to make before their performance matches their ambition in a new venue.

To be a prospector or free agent is a refreshing mindset, but you also need what I call "organization smarts." When you pursue opportunities from one organization to another, as a manager in the new economy or a specialist on demand, it makes a big difference whether you can be a quick learner and an effective player early on. *Organization Smarts* is about how you navigate that passage. It begins with understanding what the "real" organization is like that you hook up with, making it clear to others how you intend to operate, learning to anticipate their preferences, using experts to your advantage, and finding enough others to secure change. None of this guarantees success, but it certainly should improve your performance.

Recently, I read the rather plaintive comment of an executive who expressed reservations about going out on her own. She asked:

"But for those of us who are generalists . . .[h]ow does one become a free agent without a highly specific skill set?"[2] She has good reason to hesitate. Managers need a place in an organization of some kind to practice their art. Free agents don't. But her blind spot is not seeing that free agents, as well as managers on the move, and any prospector on a career path somewhere in between, need organization smarts—skills very different from the credentials that an employer or client-organization expects them to have. Graduate degrees and training certificates are valued documents. What are less easy to come by are the organization smarts that make you versatile, not just marketable, which you can use regardless of where you work or whom you work with. Prospectors need these portable skills so they can be discerning and flexible travelers prepared for any landscape, climate, or turn of events. Moving on *and* getting ahead require some dexterity. It's not just how hard you work at it, but how smart you are in doing it.

STREET SMARTS: Organization smarts have much in common with street smarts. To be streetwise is an important resource for those who live the urban life. It is not something that you are born with, and it can't be purchased on the open market. You become streetwise by observation and participation in the helter-skelter public space shared with countless strangers.

For example, do you know (1) what the best way is to catch a cab on a one-way avenue at rush hour; or (2) how a homeless man encourages passers-by to put money in his hat; or (3) what to look for in choosing an acceptable restaurant; or (4) how homeowners discourage graffiti on their block? (1) Walk in the direction of the oncoming traffic, regardless of where you want to go. If you don't, others will beat you to every cab in sight. (2) He leaves some money in the hat to reassure you that others have already found him to be a good cause. (3) See if the window has a menu posted that tells how much you'll pay and look for patrons already seated, which tells you somebody else likes the place. Nobody likes to eat in an empty restaurant. (4) They remove any graffiti as soon as it appears. Graffiti artists want more than a one-day show of their "handiwork."

The personal control that prospectors or free agents seek in their work arrangements does not spare them from the entanglements of organizational life. It makes no difference what their priorities are—money, independence, gratifying work, contributing to the public good, or using each assignment as an important career step—they still must engage with others in a complex organizational game. Even those higher-ups, who presumably have some measure of control in an organization, are not spared, especially in new decentralized environments of networked projects, cross-sector collaborations, global markets, and cyberspace itself. They cannot rely on hierarchy to secure internal and external cooperation among so many stakeholders, and their authority becomes more a crutch than a stick.[3]

The challenge for everyone, then, is not to be the master of their complicated work environments, which is fruitless, but to understand these environments better and make productive use of them. When no one controls the action fully or can dictate the outcomes, and with so many interdependent players, the organizational game becomes more interesting and more formidable. To know this is to also know that organization smarts are not a ready-made game plan with no assembly needed. Instead, they are a way of thinking and acting in any dynamic environment in which prospectors have to tailor their performance to each unique organizational context that they encounter along the way. No two organizations, just like no two games, are ever the same.

Those prospectors who succeed develop an inquiring and strategic mindset. They learn as much as they can about the new environments in which they find themselves. They do not take for granted that their values or their methodologies are trump cards in the social interaction necessary to solve problems. They learn to think *with* others rather than using positional authority or a professional credential to think *for* them. They understand that no one is in control of most problematic situations, that players' preferences conflict, and that their choices are interdependent. They are people who constantly look for new allies to build support for whatever is worth doing. They get where they are going with the help of others.

THE GAME METAPHOR: I should note here that making frequent use of the game metaphor in the chapters to follow does not mean that I use game theory as an explanatory framework. My quarrel with game theory, the formal study of strategic situations in which two or more players are interdependent, is its disregard for the specific social context within which real-world choices are made. As a consequence, the strategic advice offered by popularizations of game theory are often limited by a model that does not adequately portray the complexity of individual motivation and social interaction when a "game" is actually played in an organization.

Organization smarts acknowledge important variables that game theorists often shun or find difficult to incorporate into their models, such as the norms or precedents for how a game is played in a particular venue, the players' identities, roles, and reputations, and the inconsistency of their preferences if the game has successive rounds and develops its own unique narrative.

I also don't use the word "politics" in this book, even though it is unavoidable in organizational life. Many of us have been conditioned to dislike or condescend to politics, fueled by the cynical talk of commentators and even politicians themselves. The term "office politics" suggests messy, underhanded behavior that many people abhor. It's a shame that the practice of politics has been so debased. We really could not live without the politics of shared problem solving that goes on in every organization and community. But I won't use the term in this book because it carries too much negative baggage, which I don't have the time or wit to unpack.

The shaded boxes that appear in each chapter include games, vignettes, and minicases, which are warm-ups and practice for using your organization smarts. They put you on the ground as a participant, not as a spectator. They are open-ended exercises that you can do at home or with friends to get in shape for the actual games that go on in organizations. I have developed and tested most of these strenuous workouts, and I would love to know which ones work best for you. I can be reached at brownd@newschool.edu.

Looking Ahead

Chapter 1: Understanding the "Real" Organization

You are at a temporary disadvantage when you find yourself in a new situation in which you know little about the other players or about how their particular game is played. Each organization values different things, has different routines, and certainly has a different mix of higher-ups and lower-downs.

The chapter asks you to look beyond the official information available about an organization. The mistake that many newcomers make is to assume that someone in authority will give them all the information they need to get the job done. They fail to ask: What information is not given? What is missing? What explains how the game is played in this particular place? You cannot be an effective player until you find out how the "real" organization works.

Like a detective you should assume that a great deal of information is withheld or disputed or simply not available unless you probe. A detective, by definition, has to work at "getting information that is not readily or publicly accessible."[4] Instead of just being a consumer of the information of others, you should make your own observations and assemble your own data, finding out what is missing and what you think you need. What do you want to know that you don't know?

This chapter looks at using unofficial as well as official sources of information: What can you learn from your predecessor? Who are your supporters and detractors? What can internal reports and memoranda tell you? What do outsiders know about the organization? What do the architecture, the official literature, and "custodians" tell you about the organization's culture? What is not so visible but important in discovering that culture? What are the organization's customs, how did they arise, and why are they slow to change? What is visible and not so visible that helps to explain who has real power, who does not, and how it is shared?

Doing detective work produces more reliable answers than just relying on what other people want you to know.

Chapter 2: Establishing a Credible Reputation

When you land in an unfamiliar organization, you're not the only one with detective work to do. Your new colleagues and the networks that you become part of want to find out about you. There is little chance for you to be an effective participant until you establish a credible reputation. Your reputation in an organization is a measure of your standing with others, one that can be used for or against you in a variety of ways. Although your reputation can be victimized by innuendo, misunderstandings, or other events beyond your control, more often than not you help shape and determine what others think of you.

This chapter has you consider a number of reputation-making possibilities. What are others' first impressions of your style of play? How can your style of play be both adaptive and consistent? Why is the company you keep important? Can you walk your talk, and what does it take to live up to your reputation?

Chapter 3: Understanding What Others Want

On very busy days, I would slap the cover page of any lengthy staff memo and ask its author: "Please tell me what it says." So, then, what is this chapter about? Quite simply, if you want to get ahead, you need to anticipate, influence, and adjust to the preferences of those you work with.

Organizational life is an interesting and complicated game, and everyone who plays is dependent on everyone else. Given such interdependence, it is important to put yourself in the other person's shoes to account for preferences that are different from your own. Understanding what others want makes you a more effective player. As with any game, you should be prepared to make numerous adjustments in your play as the game progresses. You are operating in a dynamic environment that will not hold still for you to act anymore than the players in a basketball game would let you dribble the full length of a court uncontested to make a basket.

The sports analogy only goes so far, however, because a complex organizational game does not mean that someone has to win and someone has to lose. On the contrary, what works for you has to work for others, too. To put yourself in the other persons' shoes is not just for their sake, nor just for your own. First and foremost, it acknowledges your mutual dependence.

This chapter explores the importance of understanding what others want when framing problems with them, working with higher-ups, preparing for meetings, getting the commitment of others, and voting or bargaining with them.

ORGANIZATIONS: Organizations come in many different forms, and we give them various names—company, firm, nonprofit agency, public authority, etc. I prefer simply using the word "organization" through most of this book to reinforce the idea that organization smarts come in handy in any kind of workplace. I don't assume that you are planting yourself forever in the private, nonprofit, or public sector. Your talent and opportunities may take you from one to another.

Organizational hierarchies also exist in many different forms, so I just refer to "higher-ups" and "lower-downs" and only occasionally to bosses and subordinates. Every higher-up is a lower-down to some other higher-up, every lower-down is a higher-up to some other lower-down, and so on. Most prospectors start their engagements somewhere in the middle, working with both higher-ups and lower-downs. Developing advantageous relationships with all of them, regardless of a stated or unstated hierarchy, is when organization smarts come into play.

Time Out: Storytelling in Organizations

Following Chapter 3, I offer an excursion to talk candidly about how things often get done in organizational life rather than how they are portrayed.

Many storyboards in textbooks and management literature, which supposedly tell how people perform in organizations, are developed by outsiders who rely on the accounts of insiders about what goes on. Such outsiders, however, rarely comprehend the complexity of the episodes that they chronicle, and insiders often convey an impression of having had greater foresight and rationality than, in fact, was the case. With the benefit of hindsight, those who tell the story often relate a tidier account of how they accomplished whatever it is they did than how it really happened. It is all very reassuring to those who were not there, but an amiable fiction for those who actually played the game. At best, a storyboard is an abridgment of what really happened. I want to tell you about what gets left out.

My experience with problematic situations in organizations is to marvel at how well most things turned out, considering that there were a number of misunderstandings, chance encounters, mistakes, and unintended consequences that occurred along the way. You can read this excursion as a form of reassurance or with serious alarm. Either way, it offers you fresh ways of thinking about how to influence organizational outcomes.

Chapter 4: Working with Experts

If there is a quintessential underdog moment in organizational life, it is when you are a consumer of expert advice, an amateur playing with a pro. No relationship engenders more awe and antagonism than the ambivalence we feel toward our professional betters— those who know a great deal more about a particular subject than we do or who practice a specialized skill better than we can ever hope to. And just as every higher-up is a lower-down to some other higher-up, every expert is a rank amateur to some other expert. So no one is immune from such feelings.

Whatever status you have, learning to work with expert-specialists on the inside of an organization and consultants from the outside is absolutely essential. But there are no players more difficult to understand. The chapter opens up this black box to explore what accounts for their particular status, the essentials of what they do, how to determine their competence, and the possibilities for engaging all their talents, not just their expertise.

Chapter 5: Changing the Status Quo

I leave the hardest part for last—changing the status quo. You already know that it's not possible to get ahead without leaving someone behind, but when it comes to changing the status quo by moving an organization ahead, it makes little sense to leave people behind. You will be at a serious disadvantage trying to do it by yourself, and all the careless talk about "empowerment" and "win-win" is not so easy to do. You have to find what I call "enough others," enough others who see it your way, enough others to produce the needed change and to secure the change without your continued presence.

This chapter focuses on taking advantage of precipitating events that make change possible, defining a "crisis" before others do, identifying allies, and, of course, finding enough others.

BAD SCHOOLING: You would think it self-evident that it is a disadvantage to be ignorant about what others in an organization already know, to be naïve in failing to discern their interests and anticipate their preferences, or to try to go it alone. I have discovered, however, that many people do not understand their disadvantage because they have been mis-educated. Their "organization dumbs"—a combination of ignorance, naïveté, and being isolated in an organization are, in part, a consequence of too many years of bad schooling, which keeps them from performing well. This book tries to undo some of the damage.

I first saw the disadvantage of newcomer ignorance when working with government agencies caught up in the endless cycle of election campaigns, transitions, incumbency, and reelection campaigns. Inexperienced outsiders assumed roles that required substantial knowledge about how the agency worked; veteran careerists sought to curry favor without sufficient knowledge of what a "new team" wanted; and members of the new team plowed ahead without a grasp of the agency agenda they had inherited or the campaign agenda they had been charged to implement.

Later, as my graduate school teaching progressed, I realized how ill equipped students were to overcome their newcomer ignorance in those organizations in which they wanted to make their mark. Too many of them had been schooled to assume that problems were perfected by someone in authority before being offered for solution. I found that in both undergraduate and graduate courses, too much was done for students and not enough by students. They practiced their skills on problems that came ready made and well defined with enormous amounts of data. The irony is that students are shortchanged. Perfect problems and perfect answers are a serious distortion of what actually goes on in organizational problem-solving. The excessive packaging and instructions of some textbooks and courses are at odds with the trial-and-error process in which most organizational learning is grounded.

I also saw students handicapped not only by egocentricity, but also by the mistaken belief, perhaps fostered by some of their instructors, that an objective analysis of a situation should trump how it appears subjectively to others. Using a particular problem-solving method is certainly not an act of naïveté. It is a natural consequence of temperament or training. What is naïve is to assume that anyone can succeed without regard to other people's preferences or without making constant adjustments that take into account changes in those preferences.

I started to explore the problem of individual isolation and why so many people go it alone in *When Strangers Cooperate*. In a hectic and divided life with weakening social ties, they complain of individual powerlessness and malign the status quo but seem to have little hope of changing it. Again I saw the influence of bad schooling: "We establish competitive, rather than cooperative learning environments where students are tested on their individual abilities to be self-sufficient . . . [even though] our experience in organizations and communities, where little gets accomplished without collaboration with others, makes clear how few lessons of the 'real world' are included in the classroom."[5]

Implicit in my work here is the assumption that we do better for ourselves by thinking and acting with others rather than trying to be totally self-reliant. As much as we might prefer to go solo, none of us can get very far without the help of others.

Moving on *and* getting ahead—can you have both? I think you can, but like any trip, try to equip yourself ahead of time. Don't worry about where you start from; how far can you go?

I hope this book will make a difference. See what works for you. For me, the true measure is not whether you take the book along but whether you *use* it.

CHAPTER 1

Understanding the "Real" Organization

The popular saying "What you see is what you get" doesn't begin to tell enough about a new organization that you encounter. To understand the "real" organization you must go beyond just what you see. I call this *detective work*.

Think about it. Detectives enter the scene as strangers to facts that they must discover for themselves. For me, a good detective story is looking for clues and what they reveal. If the story were nothing more than the accounts of those the detective interviewed, I would quickly lose interest. What holds my interest is the detective's ability to question, surmise, and enlarge on the initial information offered. The detective knows and I know that there is still much to learn in order to solve the mystery.

15

Of course, you may prefer not having to be the detective when you enter an organization that is unfamiliar to you. Mysteries are a good read, but who wants them at the workplace? I use the detective analogy, however, because much of what you need to know about a new organization you must discover for yourself. No one is going to do it for you. The clues are everywhere, but you have to put them together in such a way that leads you to understand the real organization. And, if you are on the move and want to get ahead, you don't have a lifetime to learn. When I speak of the "real" organization, I am referring to how it actually operates, which you are not likely to find in the official literature and briefings that greet you. How do you go about looking for it? It is not as obvious as you might think, but understanding the real organization, how it really works, is indispensable if you want to make your mark early and well. Otherwise, you run the risk of being clueless and ineffective.

Using Official and Unofficial Sources of Information

Think of yourself as a detective in an unfamiliar organization, but obviously don't think of it as the scene of a crime or your new colleagues as a bunch of suspects. That will not get things off to a good start. There are, however, many reasons why your colleagues may not be forthcoming, much like a family of new in-laws or a block of new neighbors who may offer you a genuine welcome but do not think you need to know everything about them. When a newcomer is admitted to the intimate precincts of a family or neighborhood, entry is just that, a beginning.

There is much that is invisible or withheld in an organization. It is easy to forget this because initially you are offered a great deal of information—job descriptions, a table of organization policies and procedures, health insurance, pension plans, etc.—which tell you about the official organization but not necessarily about the real one. Such documentation says: "This is what we want you to know about us." You do much the same when you send out your résumé. You offer an official version of yourself, saying in so many words, "This is what I want you to know about me."

All official information is useful, assuming that it is accurate, but it is not enough. That is why those who do the hiring also interviewed you, checked your references, and made other inquiries about you so they could get behind or beyond the official story in your résumé. Similarly, you have to look around and begin to form your own picture of the organization, using both official and unofficial sources.

It makes no difference at what level you find yourself in an organization; there is lots of detective work to do. Higher-ups don't have any clear advantage over lower-downs in this respect. In fact, the more important you think that you are to an organization's operation, the more likely it is that information will be withheld from you. First and foremost, people in an organization look after themselves, so their polite greeting and official information leave out the family problems. It's an understandable precaution.

When I was asked to be the president of a small college I said "yes," but that did not entitle me to know everything I wanted to about the place. Far from it. Any search process is selective both in choosing among candidates and deciding what to tell the candidates about the organization. So I took for granted that I had to educate myself, to learn as much as I could about the college. No one was going to do it for me, and I knew that I could not be of much help to the college until I did my detective work.

Like a detective arriving on the scene, I responded to their invitation without being limited to only what they wanted me to see. I needed to walk around on my own without seeming to be ungracious. I had to find out where I was and with whom I was dealing. I started by asking questions, lots of them.

I already knew that the college was in financial trouble. That was part of the official story presented to me, but I suspected that the plot was far more complicated. Who and what was responsible for their misfortune? More important, who and what could help them get back on their feet? I didn't have a lot of time to figure this out when I looked at the dismal financials. Their disclosure was like finding the victim's body, but the real detective work was still ahead. I wanted to get beyond the official explanations.

What Can You Learn from Your Predecessor? Although I knew the financial situation of the college had become more troubling on my predecessor's watch, I wanted to understand why. When you succeed to someone else's job, it is very easy to think you can do better. That's natural, but it also makes you less interested in learning from that person. It's like meeting your new mate's former spouse—there is some curiosity but also a certain aversion.

I realized, however, that the hard part for me was realistically assessing why I had a better chance than my predecessor did to right the listing college ship before she sank altogether. I needed to know his side of the story without prejudging his performance. Others in the college—trustees, faculty, staff, alumni, and students—could certainly supply what he left out. What were his expectations when starting off in the position that now was mine? What adjustments did he have to make? What advice did he have for me? Whatever you think you already know about how your predecessor performed may be less important than what you actually learn from him.

There is another good reason for having a conversation with your predecessor. There are likely to be substantial differences in how the two of you prefer to operate, which bear little relation to the official duties that the position prescribes. What then can you learn about your predecessor's operating style and priorities as compared to your own? Everyone in the organization has to adjust to those differences, for better or worse, and you should realize that such differences affect what people think of you.

After getting to know my predecessor, I realized that those who officially welcomed me, as much as those who didn't, would need some time to adjust as they shed their responses learned under one executive and adapted to someone who was very different. At first, my predecessor was like a ghost who haunted the proceedings until the real organization got used to my way of doing things.

Who Are Your Supporters and Detractors? Knowing who composed the official organization told me nothing about who my supporters and detractors were. I had been selected by a search committee and the board of trustees, but I knew the approval was not unanimous. Whom should I make a special effort to know and learn from?

Certainly, those who initially supported me were easier to locate; they met me more than halfway. But those who hung back or seemed less forthcoming needed my early and sustained attention. Were they people whose support I needed to do my job properly? Did they have influence with those whose support was important to me? I knew that I had to cultivate both my supporters and detractors, taking neither group for granted.

For those who had opposed my selection, it helped to know why. Did they have inaccurate information about me, or was it just that they preferred someone else? Perhaps a few of them were even candidates for the job I now had. I might not be able to clear the air between us, but it was worth a try. I call it the "bear hug" approach, —keeping someone close so he can't hit you so easily. When two people in an organization have their differences, it is very easy for them to practice a kind of mutual avoidance. But this deprives each of learning more about the other, which might improve their relations. I was determined not to let that happen with anyone.

What were their ideas for what should be done? Just because they had backed the wrong horse or not been chosen themselves did not mean that their ideas should be ignored. Showing an interest in such people and tapping into their knowledge about the organization *before* it is expected of you is, in the best sense, a form of flattery. It may encourage them to share important and sensitive information, which they might otherwise withhold or overlook. If they could be moved to help me rather than be spectators, all the better for getting things done.

What Can Official Reports and Internal Memoranda Tell You?
Such documents can be surprisingly revealing. I wanted to sample what reforms had already been tried and what projects were pending. But beyond the official form of a document, I wanted to know who had written it and who had been "copied." Such information told me about other people's agendas and who was in the loop. I could not take the lead in shaping an agenda for the college without knowing who and what the competition might be. Furthermore, it can be embarrassing to recommend changes that you think are new to an organization only to find that they have already been proposed or tried.

Such detective work also alerted me to what I might expect from those who tried to win me over to agendas that had already been rejected or shelved by others. Nothing prevented me from helping to resurrect such proposals, but I wanted to know what others already knew about why the proposals had been rejected. The official and unofficial versions of "why" can tell you a lot about the capacity of an organization for change and who the important players are likely to be in helping or hindering what you think needs to be done.

I also looked at the official minutes of meetings—committees, trustees, advisory groups—to get a sense of what such groups had accomplished. What was the range of their interests? Even though formal minutes are often sanitized to obscure the give and take of organizational life, they sometimes reveal more than they intend. I looked for clues to help me understand who promoted change, who opposed it, and why? How did they settle their differences— by someone pulling rank, by voting, or by repeatedly putting off any resolution at all?

Since the college had encountered rough financial seas, what did recent grievances and turnover data tell me about the morale of the faculty, of the staff, of the students? Due to the financial instability, were there unresolved personnel matters or measures threatened that I should know about and act on rather than letting them fester?

What Do Outsiders Know About Your Organization? I had to take into account official audits and pending accreditation visits. What impact were they having on the college? What did their findings or scheduled visits tell me about our work and what needed to be done? Often an organization prepares feverishly for such visits and responds politely to such reports only to then ignore their findings and recommendations. Sometimes there is good reason for doing so if the recommendations are unrealistic. The official exchange between external critics and internal players, however, is an important dialogue to study, as well as trying to learn about the unofficial conversations that preceded and followed it.

The opinions of constituencies external to an organization are also important. Beyond their official greeting on my schedule, I found time for a number of unscheduled visits with residents of the town, neighbors of the campus, local alumni, and elected officials. I discovered that faculty and staff concerns were far different from those in the community. I needed to hear both in order to develop my priorities, especially where they were in conflict. I made sure to have one-to-one meetings with key players who were both on and beyond the campus. The large, getting-to-know-you, official meeting in an auditorium has its symbolic purpose, but vital information is better extracted from more discreet and candid conversations.

With all of this reconnaissance, I began to connect the lines between and among those I met. I discovered who had sponsored whom for a job, who "went way back together" in the college or the larger community, who "could not sit in the same room together," why some department chairs worked well with their colleagues and why some did not, who the unofficial leaders were and who their followers were, who mentored whom, and so on.

Naturally, much of what you originally learn from official and unofficial sources has to be amended and revised as you go along, but it is of great initial help in putting together pieces of information, which no one will necessarily volunteer without your asking.

TRI-CITY COLLEGE: Now imagine that you are the new vice president for development at Tri-City College. What official and unofficial sources of information should you pursue?

Tri-City College will soon have an important visitor, Dr. Louis Steadman, the chairperson of the Mid-States Accreditation Association (MSAA). He will be returning to Tri-City, a private college, to determine whether it can be removed from MSAA's "watch list" of those institutions considered "financially unstable." Such a finding was made a year ago when Tri-City was reaccredited, provided there was a demonstrable improvement in its financial condition.

Everyone knows that the MSAA finding is not helping the perception of funders, donors, prospective students, and faculty candidates when trying to decide whether to invest their dollars or futures in the college. The sooner Tri-City is off Dr. Steadman's "watch list," the better.

But Tri-City's president has suddenly resigned for health reasons before having a chance to do much of anything to get Tri-City back in the black. He had run the college almost single-handedly for eighteen years. Certainly all money matters of any consequence had been in his hands, both the getting and the spending, and he loved to do both. He personally pursued all major gifts and maintained close and cordial relations with practically every donor of consequence, whether an alum, foundation, or business executive. You were hired by the former president, but he resigned before you even started your job, and you are playing catch-up with all that needs to be learned about the college and its donor base and prospects.

It is clear to the provost and acting president, Dee D'Alembert, that she needs a lot of help in the development effort. Trained as a biologist and in her mid-fifties, she knows that fund-raising is not her strong suit. She is a candidate, however, for the presidency of Tri-City and knows that Dr. Steadman will be returning soon. She immediately turned to you, an M.B.A. graduate who has moved up the career ladder of institutional development, changing jobs three times in five years.

D'Alembert is extremely cautious by nature, and, being only the acting president, she has hesitated to take actions that might be second-guessed by the search committee or undone in the event someone else is ultimately chosen

instead of her. What the cautious D'Alembert has been willing to do is review with you two of the projects of the former
president.

First, she told you about the plan to establish an Elder
Hostel (a residential, cultural enrichment program for senior
citizens) on campus each summer as a source of revenue.
The former president left the project in the hands of an advisory board of senior citizens from the local area who had lob-
bied him and now were in charge, given his departure.
According to D'Alembert, there is a great deal of conflict in
their ranks but, nonetheless, they have drawn up a very size-
able budget and are acting on their own, largely ignoring the
provost with whom they have never established good relations.

The Elder Hostel plan calls for air-conditioning all the
dormitories and paying very healthy stipends to faculty
members willing to take part at summer pay levels, which
D'Alembert thinks is excessive. The advisory board argues
that the faculty are reluctant to take part in the program
unless they are generously compensated. D'Alembert told
you that the faculty always try to hold out for more, whatever the proposal, but she hesitates to get more involved,
given her relations with those on the advisory board, many
of whom have made provision for Tri-City in their wills. They
are largely wealthy retired couples who have moved to the
area and made the college and the Elder Hostel program
their consuming project.

Next, D'Alembert briefed you on the "New Horizons"
summer school, an arts program for tri-city area high school
students, some of them from minority neighborhoods, with
the object of not only enriching their lives, but perhaps of

steering them toward Tri-City as a place to matriculate when they are ready for college. The program has been primarily funded by Shu Gates, a wealthy trustee and chair of the presidential search committee, who has made it his pet project.

D'Alembert, however, thinks the program has very little support from other trustees or the faculty. Furthermore, very few of those teenagers taking part have subsequently enrolled at Tri-City, and the expense of keeping the campus open and the cost of extra staffing has made the program a drain on the college's budget. Last summer, excessive damage in the dormitories, now coupled with the expectation of Elder Hostel visitors coexisting with New Horizons students, is causing D'Alembert great concern.

Looking for the Culture

Does the organization have a culture? It is an important question, but before you can answer it, you have to know what to look for. Think of a culture as something that is shared by a number of people. You and I can not individually possess a culture, but we can be part of one and help maintain and contribute to it. At the heart of a culture is an agreement about what is important to a group whose size can range from a department in an organization (what is usually referred to as a "subculture") to the organization itself, to a neighborhood, a region, a nation-state, or even one with global dimensions.

The size of the group is less important than whether there is widespread agreement about what is important. And this is where culture can be elusive. Not all groups can agree on what is important. Some people may work in an organization where they share nothing more than a 9-to-5 job for a paycheck at the end of the month. They share common space and common tasks, but there is little agreement about what is important to them *as a group*. We know what is important to each of them individually—to come to work, do the job, and go home—but that is hardly a culture. Culture in an organization is about what is special to it. A 9-to-5 mentality is hardly special. You can find it anywhere. What does the organization, and the people who comprise it, share, that you, the newcomer, cannot possess alone? There you may find its culture.

Whatever of significance that you find your colleagues share, to be a culture it has to affect the myriad ways they carry on the daily life of the organization. For a culture to exist there must be evidence of it in how people behave. If a new CEO says: "From now on this company will unfailingly be customer friendly in everything we say or do," the statement itself does not create a culture. Unless those in the organization adjust their behavior so that is believable to customers, no higher-up can remake the workplace. Culture in an organization cannot just be imposed. It takes a willing consent as expressed in how people choose to behave. When you find some official statements of the organization's "culture," the measure of whether it exists comes from listening and watching what your colleagues actually say and do.

It takes time for any culture to develop, to grow roots. Once established, it is often difficult to change or uproot. You are likely to find a culture or subcultures in the organization where there is a stability of membership that has allowed for testing and modifying the shared assumptions that now animate it. For someone like you who is not rooted, a strong culture may seem unnecessary or even threatening to how you like to operate. Nonetheless, be prepared to engage the culture you find—there is no way to avoid it other than leaving the organization for another.

So, first off as a detective, what is the evidence that a culture exists in the organization? What are the clues? The easy part is looking for the visible evidence that is already available. The hard part is ascertaining what is not immediately visible—the shared assumptions of those you work with. If little is *shared*, tangible or intangible, then there may be no culture to speak of—a kind of bus terminal where those who use it have no common destination.

What Is Visible?

The Architecture.   Look at the architecture of where you work. Does it make a statement that is coherent about what the organization values?[1] When IBM moved into its new corporate headquarters in 1997, the building was a radical departure from the old IBM. Lou Gerstner, the company's chief who helped move the old IBM into a new networked era, made sure the building design offered an open floor plan where collaboration and innovation could flourish. There were lots of places set aside as temporary work stations and for working get-togethers. On the same corporate property sat the empty, former HQ, with its ubiquitous private offices and the absence of adequate wiring for office networking. Both HQ buildings made different cultural statements about what was valued and what was not.

Many buildings, of course, say little about their owners or prime tenants. But where and how parts of the organization are lodged may speak volumes. What department is given the most favorable space? What does that say about what the organization values? What activities, aside from work, are valued? What kind of amenities—courtyards, plazas, terraces, cafeterias, fitness rooms, day care centers, parking lots—are provided for employees, for customers?

Where are visitors greeted and what does that space say about the culture? Perhaps, like me, you have visited organizations where your presence seems to be positively resented. No one has time for you, or they ask you to wait for someone who does and then leave you in an anteroom that looks like a holding pen for first offenders.

First impressions are important, and an organization that has a strong culture wants you to know about it. You can learn a lot about a workplace in its reception area. If there is no greeting at the front door, what must the rest of the place be like? Perhaps it is a busy warren of overachievers with no time for pleasantries with strangers. A culture is what members of a group value, not necessarily what you and I would want them to value.

The Official Literature.   Pick up the official literature on the reception table. What does the organization say it values? There is bound to be some general statement to that effect. Here your "skunk" antenna should be turned on just as it is when you watch a TV ad or read public relations copy in a newspaper. Does the organization's statement about itself correspond to what you have learned so far?

The organization's annual report may tell a productivity story, a financial story, or perhaps a strategic vision story, but such official literature may also weave in the basic story of the organization—its founding and its achievements. Every organization has a history. What does the telling say about what the organization values? In the telling, there may be some myths, which take liberties with what actually happened. Nonetheless, they say a great deal about the organization's culture. After all, what is shared by members of a group does not have to be objectively true as long as they honor it in their everyday work lives. Large myths are usually more influential than small truths, anyway.

For example, as the new president of an old, nineteenth-century college, I wanted to know about its heroes and legends. What did their stories tell me about the limits and possibilities at the college? As a newcomer, I could not ignore the history even if I had wanted to. I knew that I had to work within a given culture that the institution's heroes and legends helped to shape as they faced their own perils that were not unlike the college's financial predicament that I encountered.

Custodians. When looking to see whether a culture exists, see if you can learn from an unofficial leader, or someone I call a "custodian," about what the group-at-large values are. Such people usually are long-standing employees who have earned a reputation for being the personification of the organization itself. They often reach out to newcomers, like you, explaining in a friendly but forceful way, "This is how we do things around here."

Custodians tell stories about important episodes in the life of the organization. They seem to be utterly secure and confident in what they know. Their co-workers defer to them, "Oh, talk to Sam about that. He knows everything there is to know about the founding family." Or, "You should ask Helen. She can tell you how that practice got started. She is an unimpeachable source for whatever you want to know." Such employees may not have important titles or official functions that would draw you to them, but they have acquired a central role in explaining the organization to those who ask or are in need of some guidance.

If such people exist in your organization, there is likely to be some kind of culture. Custodians speak for others, for the group, and you do well to listen and heed what they say. They certainly make your detective work easier because they fill in so much that is not made explicit in the architecture or the literature of the place. Like village elders, they can tell you about the wisdom or foolishness of the official leaders. They can measure what they know about you against what they know about the organization and, like a good tailor, tell you how good or how bad the fit is. In many ways, finding the custodians of your organization's culture is finding the culture itself and what it is about.

What Is Not So Visible?

What if the architecture and the literature tell you very little about the organization, and there is no custodian to be found on the premises? Perhaps there is no culture—always a possibility. And yet within particular departments, sections, or other units, you sense that groups share particular values that are not found elsewhere in the organization. Now you have to cross over from looking for the visible evidence, which is available to everyone, to identifying unspoken assumptions and the possibility of "subcultures."

I have said that culture is what people share, but it is obviously more than the space and time together that they have in common. When a number of people agree on what they value, what they consider important, that agreement is not necessarily made explicit, even though it substantially influences their behavior.[2] When a subculture is embedded in a particular unit, those who work there usually take it for granted. Their assumptions about what is important to the group do not require discussion. Their behavior confirms on a daily basis the underlying agreement that they share.

For example, if your colleagues prefer to enhance their productivity by collaboration, rather than competition, that becomes an assumption that each of them is entitled to make about how things should be done in their unit and an expectation about how people should behave toward one another. Everyone may be expected to help those who are less computer literate, or not to compete for individual bonuses but instead split whatever comes their way at the end of the year with other members of the group. Such an unspoken agreement and the assumptions and expectations that flow from it may not be immediately visible to a newcomer.

A subculture can be hidden from a stranger's view because it thrives independently of whatever "official" values prevail in the whole organization. The subculture may even arise and draw its strength from being in opposition to how the majority in an organization thinks and behaves. To understand the real organization, which may have thriving subcultures, it is not enough to rely on the official line. Does the behavior of your colleagues tell another story? Do they have recurring complaints about how the place is organized and how it pursues its daily business? How do they react to a new policy, treat a visitor, talk to one another in meetings or over coffee? Are there significant differences in behavior depending on what department or section you are observing? Does each have a subculture operating that reflects a tacit agreement about how to behave? Do the identities of gender, ethnicity, or education level distinguish one from another?

To understand the real organization requires that you determine what makes each group tick that you are part of or work with. It is possible that a custodian may tell you up front, but otherwise you have to piece the clues together for yourself.

BRASH VENTURE, INC.: Here's a workplace problem to practice on as the new administrative director at Brash Venture, Inc.

It had been a memorable day, your first at Brash Venture, Inc. Not one, not two, but three of your new colleagues asked for your advice about problems they were having with their subordinates or with the firm in general. They hired you to be the administrative director, a position newly created to help the firm manage its growth and tame its disorder. You were told: "We'll make the money. You look after the store."

Propped up on your couch at home with a bowl of popcorn, you reviewed in your mind the day's conversations.

You could see that Spandex, a leading young partner in the firm, was livid. "I cannot understand that new associate of mine. I gave Lisa a job to do, and what happens? She checks back with me on every little detail. Am I a piece of flypaper? Yesterday I was having a miserable time trying to get everything done so I called Lisa in and said, 'Do me a favor. Call the Zimmer Fund and tell them I can't make their meeting but that I've asked you to stand in for me.'

"Simple instructions, right? Then the rest of the day, she's popping back in with, 'Do you want me to bring up our reservations about the co-venture idea with them when we meet?'

"And I told her, 'No, Lisa, the meeting is supposed to be about their proposal to use Delta Bank if we decide to do a co-venture.'

"An hour later in she comes. 'Do I say anything about the Pennypacker deal if they ask?' "And I tell her, 'Don't worry, they won't ask.'

"Then, just when I am totally overwhelmed with other things, Lisa sticks her head in and asks me if I want her to sign off on using Delta Bank if the numbers look OK. 'Of course! Tell them you have my authority to do so. Bring the work-up back to me, and we'll go over it together.' How's she going to learn unless there's feedback, right?"

Spandex paced back and forth. "You know, Lisa is a very talented person, but I just can't get her to take the ball and run with it. She likes working with me. I'm sure of that. She told someone in the office that she thinks I'm the brightest dealmaker in the firm and sees me as a sure ticket for promotion. But unless she starts showing some independence, I can't do anything for her. She has to do her share of deals for this firm. I just don't have the time to hold her hand. Her performance has really forced me to hedge my bets, so I give copies of some of my deal work-ups to young Tyler and some to, what's his name, Shea, just in case Lisa doesn't come through. I can't afford to lose a deal because she doesn't have the wherewithal to get the job done on her own."

Later you found Speedo, another key partner, also in the dumps. "Oh boy, have I screwed up. I thought that I hired a young dynamo. Perfect for the job as my assistant. Right? Wrong! He is a disaster. I gave Wyatt half of my finance deals to work on. Half, can you imagine that? I had such confidence in him. It was going to give me more time with my kids. Finally, I had an associate who could free me up from my sixteen-hour workdays. So what happens? Wyatt does an apparently half-baked analysis on the Airport deal, then sits down with my counterpart at Mercury Securities and blows it entirely.

"Mercury calls me and says, 'What have you sent us? Your guy is over his head. And when we objected to his numbers, he pulled a tantrum and stormed out of the meeting. If you want to do deals with us, you'd better send a grownup next time—like yourself.'

"I just don't get it. Wyatt couldn't be nicer with me, and then he goes out and plays Attila the Hun. He seems to have a grasp for the deals when we talk them over, but something is missing when he sits down with those outside the firm—maybe it's a lack of good judgment. Some people have it; some people don't. Right? I still think Wyatt can be a super dealmaker. Unfortunately, very few others seem to agree. The guy's confidence will be shattered if I take my deals away from him. But if I don't?"

When you met with Brash, the founder of the firm, he seemed pleased but puzzled. "We have a terrific group of players here. Spandex and Speedo are beating their brains out. They remind me so much of myself when I first established the firm. I suppose that's why I eventually brought them in—bright, eager, willing to take risks.

"I know that they could handle even more deals for us, but our older clients look to me. They are aware that I know the history of every deal we ever made, and the ins and outs with every competing firm in the business. There are some things that they think only I can do. But with my heart bypass surgery, what was once exhilarating—to be on top of it all—now wears me down. I know I'm ultimately accountable to the board and our clients, but I wish there was a better way."

Brash went on. "Spandex and Speedo and, I imagine, their associates, are in constant orbit. We rarely get a chance to see each other except to finalize deals, that sort of thing. They probably wonder when I'm going to let go of the strings, but don't you see how hard that is under the circumstances? I guess the reason that we hired you is that we need a fresh perspective. What do you see that we don't?"

Does Brash Venture have a culture? What do you see that they don't?

Learning the Customs

An organization may or may not have a culture. Getting a number of people to share the same values and assumptions is not easy or always possible. Having customs, the routines and unwritten rules of the workplace, is more common. But what are they?

The routines may be obvious—taking a coffee break at 10:30 A.M., getting approval for any new hire, or observing a network protocol for sending e-mail, but the unwritten rules may not be so obvious—avoiding certain tables that are reserved for particular groups in the cafeteria, sending any prospective employee to a particular "custodian" for a little chat, or declining software upgrades unless everyone in the unit gets them.

What is important about all of the routines and unwritten rules in a workplace, obvious or not, is what they tell you about the real organization. If culture is an agreement about what people value in their organizational life together, then many of their routines and unwritten rules are agreements about how they have chosen to *coordinate* that organizational life.

As a newcomer, you inherit certain routines and unwritten rules particular to the organization. Its customs are slow to change, and, as with culture, you have to work within them. Whether you like it or not, they clarify what makes the organization distinctive from others that you have known. Learning quickly how to get things done that mesh with the existing order can help you make an early contribution and may be a fair measure of what you can expect to eventually accomplish.

How Do Organizational Customs Arise?

A routine or unwritten rule in an organization is usually the consequence of people wanting to coordinate their individual behavior for the sake of better relations and performance. Try the following exercise to understand better how some bottom-up routines originate by doing it with a group of colleagues.

For each coordination choice below, *the best choice depends on what each of you think the choice of the others is likely to be.* Just one rule: No communication. Everyone has to guess or reason on their own what "focal point" they think the others will choose.[3]

1. Ask each of them to choose a restaurant where everyone can meet for dinner next week.

2. Ask each of them for which night the reservation should be made.

3. Ask each of them for what time the reservation should be made.

4. Ask each of them what the dress code should be.

When you are finished, compare your choices with those of your colleagues. In each instance, did a majority of you make the same choice? Call that a one-time coordination solution that can become controlling by simple repetition. If you and your colleagues were to do the exercise again, each of you would probably choose whatever a majority chose in the first round.

A bottom-up routine can originate in the same way. For instance, the effort level in processing certain paperwork might have originated by the example of a senior employee, and others followed his lead; or the timing of coffee breaks may be solely due to when hot pastries are delivered to a particular floor; or co-workers started covering for each other after the starting hour was moved up thirty minutes and disrupted the schedules of certain working mothers and fathers. Such routines may not represent everyone's preference of how to do something, but it works on the basis of "majority rules." That is why newcomers often look disdainfully at such customs because they seem arbitrary to someone who has not yet experienced their benefits or discovered the reasons they are used.

It may be difficult for prospectors, who have a strong sense of self, to understand why a routine or unwritten rule that prescribes a particular kind of conduct should be a significant force in any organization. An organization custom, however, is a well-worn path. No one has to clear a way, everyone assumes that it originated to serve some purpose, and more often than not it gets people where they want to go. The original reason for the path often gets lost, but that makes little difference. We "emulate what others have found reason to do."[4] And that seems good enough for most people, who rarely ask, "Why are we doing this?" They trust that question has been settled. If, however, you can discover the reason, it may help you evaluate just how good a path it really is.

Consider how an organization puts together an annual budget. More than likely, it is an incremental process in which budget allocations to the respective departments or units are carried over from year to year with only minor adjustments. The annual budget process represents a kind of truce among conflicting interests in the organization. The unwritten rule is not to open old wounds about who gets how much except at the margins.[5] If newcomers understand this unwritten rule as regulating the distribution of an organization's limited resources, they are not likely to make enemies early on by expecting more than they are entitled to under the existing budget truce. Eventually, they may have good reason or a compelling need to get off that beaten path, but at least they will have learned what the risks are and why their colleagues may not follow.

Why Are Organizational Customs Slow to Change?

When you suggest an alternative way of doing something in an organization, someone may very well say: "That won't work here." What your colleagues know, and you may not yet understand, is that a custom for them is robust—no one has reason to change it. It is like driving on the right side of the road. Why would anyone prefer to defy that rule? You could get killed. Other routines may be more fragile if people in the organization still entertain alternatives, just as drivers do when they have the option to change lanes on an expressway, and their driving behavior becomes less predictable, less coordinated.

Routines and unwritten rules spare those in an organization from having to think too much. That's not all bad. The thinking is presumed to be done by higher-ups. The routines and rules coordinate the actions of everyone else. Whatever an organization does for a living, the idea is to give guidance to newcomers and reassurance to veterans about what works—the rules of thumb for pricing products or sizing up sales prospects or evaluating employee productivity. Without common benchmarks, there is a lot of confusion if the left hand doesn't know what the right hand is doing.

Routines and unwritten rules that are self-enforcing also spare the cost and time of monitoring compliance. James March points out that "The more a particular rule is used, the better becomes the performance using that rule, so the more likely it is that the rule will be reinforced by experience. The more a rule is reinforced, the more likely it is to be used. This positive feedback loop produces considerable competence in using a current rule."[6]

Routines and rules are especially important in large organizations, which need more coordination. In a large organization, people come and go, but the routines and rules don't. Some unwritten rules, of course, simply originate with higher-ups or become "official" in an organization when they are adopted by higher-ups. Once a routine or rule becomes established in a large organization, just plain inertia may set in, preventing it from being changed. A custom that was originally introduced as an optimal solution to a problematic situation may often outlive its usefulness and become suboptimal. Circumstances change in the organization, but the routine or rule does not. Unlike the newcomer, veterans of the organization may pay little or no attention to how well their customary ways of doing things actually work. Such customs simply persist because no one thinks to do otherwise.

You may find that a custom in an organization is only a coping mechanism. Circumstances change, but the rule continues because it is just too time consuming to get people to change how they do things. Like those who have waited their turn in a line, your colleagues have become invested in whatever coordinates their behavior. They are reluctant to accept some untested substitute, to get out of line, so to speak, with no certain prospect of improving the situation. Regardless, then, of what you think, the advantage for them of adhering to an unwritten rule is its predictability, which helps them plan their activities and coordinate their respective interests, not an easy thing to do and not easily undone by you or anyone else. If you did that dinner exercise with a group of your colleagues and it actually became a custom you shared at the same place on the same weeknight at the same time with the same dress code, it would probably endure even if one of you dropped out.

Like a new member of a team, you have to learn how its members play the game. Don't assume that they want to learn new ways of doing things to add to their repertoire. Their response is likely to be: "Listen, do you want to play on our team?" Such a question is both an invitation and a subtle rebuke if you are seen as someone who does not want to play by their rules. Job security and the chance of promotion leads many of them to abide by the unwritten rules of the organization rather than trying to change them. This should not necessarily preclude your questioning certain routines and rules, but you should understand why many others don't.

THE PARTNERSHIP FUND: As the new executive director of the Partnership Fund, a nonprofit organization in Gotham, you recently hired a CFO to help bring some fiscal discipline to an organization that has perhaps bitten off more than it can chew. The Partnership Fund's mission is to devote its resources to the problems and needs of the City of Gotham and its residents.

At present, the Fund staff is largely divided into five teams pursuing projects aimed at improving the quality of performance and the productivity of city government. The staff projects include: (1) developing a methodology, called "scorecard," to rate the relative cleanliness of streets, parks, and playgrounds; (2) applying new medical protocols for use at city-owned hospitals; (3) developing an information system for monitoring the progress of children in foster homes; (4) streamlining the procedure to put housing acquired by the city in tax delinquency proceedings under interim lease and eventual sale to tenant associations; and (5) developing standards for determining the need for home health care in individual cases and the amount of services required.

Yesterday, the new CFO urged you to establish a new budgeting process. Current team projects have run on too long and incurred higher costs than originally contemplated. He argued that the Fund would be unable to pursue new initiatives because the turnover of key players in Gotham's client-agencies had jeopardized timely payments to the Fund and thrown the Fund back on its own resources to support the existing staff teams working on the projects. He wants better internal planning of the time and cost associated with any ongoing or proposed project.

This morning the CFO asked for your approval of a draft e-mail to all of the Fund's staff:

"In anticipation of the coming fiscal year, which is just four months away, we want to generate sufficient information and discussion to make thoughtful reallocations in our operating budget. We can't just take a look at incremental changes, up or down, in budget lines. That's not enough. We have to measure expenditures against known objectives. A traditional budget is organized around functions, personnel, and maintenance, not objectives. The most rational way to cut costs and keep them under control is to agree on what matters most to this nonprofit organization and to make sure the expenditures reflect its priorities.

The new budgeting process that we want to put in place will work as follows:

1. After discussion among its members, each project team will analyze the effects of conducting its project at various levels of funding;

2. The five project leaders will then meet to rank all current projects using the Fund's overall objectives to compare the relative merits of each project; and

3. We will then discuss with the entire staff, and eventually with the Fund's board of trustees, the composite ranking generated by the project leaders.

Such a ranking process should tell us where budget reallocations should be made—higher ranking projects getting full funding, lower ranking projects being curtailed or phased out. We hope that we can complete the team analyses, project leader rankings, and our discussions within the next three months. We ask that each project leader meet with the CFO as soon as possible so that the new budgeting process can be scheduled to everyone's satisfaction."

Do you approve the proposed e-mail to the staff?

Figuring Out the Power Relations

Power relations are bound to exist in any organization, but they are rarely discussed. For many, power is a provocative concept that is difficult to discuss openly. Like sexual relations, power relations are ubiquitous but essentially a private matter. Most of us don't talk willingly about either.

For some people, the idea of power is even distasteful. They would prefer it not to exist at all because, by definition, power creates inequality in the workplace. But, like it or not, power relations do exist, and you need to learn about them if you are to understand the real organization. Since power is a delicate and controversial subject, you have to look for both visible and not so visible evidence, just as you do in probing the existence or mysteries of workplace culture and its unwritten rules.

What Is Visible?

When we say someone has power over us, it often means that by virtue of a privileged position they can influence our behavior whether we like it or not. There is an explicit or visible power relation between those who are in such positions and those who are not. Positional power in the official power structure or hierarchy is relatively easy to find in an organization. Look for those with the title on the door, the large office space, and the perks that go with it. You don't need to be a detective; just keep your eyes open.

"Perks" is short for perquisites, which one dictionary defines as "privileges . . . incidental to regular salary or wages."[7] We all know perks when we see them, although many remain hidden so as not to provoke comparisons of what some people in an organization have and what others do not. Perks for the "haves" may include things as mundane as free newspaper subscriptions, custom-designed stationery, and a designated parking space in the company lot. Perks may also include special computer software and hardware, the use of an exclusive dining room, and first-class airline seats.

Watch for the perks when someone gets a new office. Credenzas appear, chandeliers tinkle as new coats of paint are applied, and a private bathroom is outfitted. Colleagues may enter and nod approvingly and then hurry back to their offices to hatch their own redecorating schemes. A great deal of time can be spent on floor plans in an organization. Sometimes, the larger the new office, the less its occupant has to do. It is a variant of Parkinson's law—offices expand to fill the time available to walk around in them and admire the heft of the draperies, impressive but little used electronic gadgetry, and carpets so thick your shoes don't show. And don't forget to look for the perk of a company-owned car, which provides a literal power trip. The company-owned car is a particularly potent status symbol if it comes with an assigned driver, but the driver is for more than just appearance. It is impossible to use a reading lamp in the backseat if you have to drive the car yourself.

Favoring certain people with better office space, automobiles, and drivers may also say something about the culture—what is valued in the organization when such perks are conspicuously visible. What is not so visible is the status the perks confer and how people use such status to influence others who might not otherwise be impressed. As a prospector, you may find a colleague's preoccupation with perks to be a bit looney. They probably mean far less to people like you who don't plan to stay long enough in any organization to collect them. But keep in mind that those who stake their claim long enough in an organization consider perks a reward for loyal service and something they and others use to compare each other's standing in the organization over the long run. Take away employees' perks and you take away their status.

Perks are not trifles. They are important symbols to the veteran in an organization.

You can find a hundred different ways that power relations are expressed in an organization between those who have the formal authority and those who do not. Who calls for a meeting? In whose office is the meeting held? Who sits at the head of the table or at the center? Who can leave without explaining why? Who never answers his or her phone? Who gets phone calls returned and e-mail replies—promptly? Who enters and leaves the workplace on whatever schedule suits their convenience? Such privileges are less tangible than perks but obvious enough to everyone in the workplace who finds it necessary to accommodate to them.

There are always those in an organization who like to throw their weight around just for the sake of distinguishing the haves from the have-nots. But the more able practitioners on whom authority is conferred are more subtle. They understand that power relations should not be exploited, and they use authority artfully for legitimate purposes. In this sense, they earn their authority by how they treat others rather than merely relying on the positional power that the organization has already granted them. They only assert their positional power when they need to remind someone who has forgotten who has it and who doesn't.

What Is Not So Visible?

What about those who have little or no formal authority but who nonetheless are influential in the organization? How did they acquire power in their relations with others? Here you cannot rely on the visible evidence of big offices, big budgets, or big meetings. You should take the time to discover why certain people are especially valued in the organization and what they do that gives them a power base. Who has the expertise, the charisma, or the reputation for getting things done? Who has the resources or is part of a network? Who do you depend on, and who depends on you?

Expertise can be knowing more or doing better what others don't know or can't do as well. It is an enormous source of individual influence. There is no denying that knowledge is power, and those on whom an organization relies for financial projections, technological fixes, research and development, legal advice, and any number of other specialties wield considerable power. It is not that they are indispensable, either on payroll or as free agents, but their knowledge and skills are.

Charisma is a personal trait that some people have and some do not. The expression "I know it when I see it" best describes how you find those with charisma in an organization. They have the looks or the charm, or both, to attract attention. For those so gifted, charisma gives them an advantage in persuading others to do their bidding. Of course, charisma is often found in those who are higher-ups, and it may explain why they have advanced in the organization.

A good *reputation* is a coalescing of opinion about someone that gives her the opportunity to use such hearsay to her advantage. If someone's reputation is suspect or negative, then it limits what power the person might otherwise have. A reputation can enhance or diminish someone's influence in an organization. It is a matter of perception. If others think that you have influence, then you do. And if they think you don't have influence, then you will find it harder to acquire.

The *resources* of an organization are always limited and contested. For a person to have some discretion on how certain resources are divided—new computer hardware, additional personnel lines—gives that person, at least temporarily, certain power over others who compete for those resources. Obviously those with positional authority are in command of such resources, but it is often their assistants, lacking any official power of their own, who act as resource gatekeepers and thereby acquire greater standing in an organization. That is why it is only natural to cultivate someone's assistant who plays such a role. Both of you understand that your power relations are not measured by seniority or salary.

Network power, unlike reputation, is really not an individual asset but one that is shared among a number of people who exert their influence by maintaining communication with each other. Such networks can be a mix of internal and external players who can improve their individual standing by being part of one. Power relations are shaped to some extent by what people do for each other through the networks they share and actively cultivate. And, as already noted, if a particular network believes that someone is an expert, has charisma, or is a gatekeeper to important organizational resources, then such reputation-building confers even greater influence on that person.

Interdependence is unavoidable, as most of us operate in increasingly decentralized environments in which project-centered teams and collaboration across units create temporary but important interdependencies among the players involved. Positional authority is of less consequence because there is far less centralized control, and there are fewer distinctions between higher-ups and lower-downs as the knowledge capital of individuals at every level of an organization shapes how things get done. Interdependence extends to those we participate with in electronic knowledge exchanges, collaborative research, joint ventures, cross-sector and cross-cultural partnerships, coalitions, and alliances. If someone is dependent on you, it gives you a measure of power and influence in relation to that person. Similarly, whom do you need to get something done? Who can stymie your effort?[8] Which players in all of these cross-cutting undertakings and networks are critical to your success?

NEW WORLDS MUSEUM: As the new associate director of the New Worlds Museum, how would you describe the power relations in the following vignette?

Bernie Hudson and Maria Sands love start-up projects. They founded Sci-Tech, Inc., which has grown from a small enterprise in Bernie's garage to a world leader in satellite communications and other high tech fields. Bernie and Maria then turned their entrepreneurial talents to founding the New Worlds Museum, a place where young people could learn about the astounding breakthroughs of knowledge-based industries.

The Museum is temporarily housed in a former post office building downtown, while a capital campaign is being organized to eventually fund a state-of-the-art interactive museum to be built on property adjacent to Sci-Tech that Bernie and Maria have donated. After four years in the post office, the Museum now wants to build and market a place where young people can come to have a hands-on experience with the future. There would be exhibits on space, microelectronics, biotechnology, and robotics.

The local establishment of Pioneer Valley, a fast-growing, high-tech urban corridor that the Museum serves, is very excited about the project. It would be a boon to tourism and the local schools and would, it is hoped, attract new donors from the enormous wealth generated by Pioneer Valley's rapid development. Until now much of that new wealth, except for Bernie and Maria, has not done its civic share.

At least one board member of the Museum, however, is unhappy with how the project is progressing. Cleo Walker, a community activist, sees too much of Bernie Hudson's hand in the Museum's affairs. Bernie insisted at the outset that

Frank Pruitt be the executive director of the enterprise, which was readily accepted by the then-fledgling board. Pruitt had been a fairly high-level manager at Sci-Tech who, Walker later learned, was put on the Museum's payroll soon after sexual harassment allegations were made against Pruitt by his executive assistant at Sci-Tech. The allegations were dropped when Pruitt left Sci-Tech.

Whatever did or did not happen at Sci-Tech, Walker doesn't like how Pruitt always defers to Hudson on matters large or small concerning the Museum. Bernie Hudson has served as chair of the board but steered the Museum's affairs through Pruitt and has often neglected to consult with his eight board colleagues. The majority of the original board members accepted this arrangement, but as new members joined and the board expanded to fifteen, Walker, now the chair herself, believes that the Hudson-Pruitt alliance is seen as an end run around those who are eager to be activists, just like herself, in the Museum's affairs.

When Maria Sands told Walker that she intended to resign from the board, citing other pressing responsibilities, Walker sensed that even Hudson's copartner in the Museum venture was getting tired of its being Bernie's show. Maria never cared much for Pruitt and told Walker as much at a board meeting recently. Cleo Walker knew that the fund-raising campaign to build on the new site would be in some jeopardy if there were more board defections or an attitude of "let Bernie do it." Bernie thought of the campaign as his "baby," and he wanted to be in control to ensure its success. Seeing himself as a visionary and the Museum as an expression of that vision, Hudson thought of himself as the only one who could make it a reality.

As the new associate director of the Museum, you are alarmed about Maria Sands' pending resignation from the board. You consider Sands your mentor and someone who can deal with Frank Pruitt when he is too domineering over the staff or too deferential to Bernie Hudson. You assume that you were recruited by Sands, in part, to be the cofounder's eyes and ears. You bring very little management experience to the Museum, but its small staff, nonetheless, has already turned to you for support and guidance when Pruitt leaves them out of planning exercises, budget sessions, and board meetings, and shows his fierce temper if anyone approaches Bernie Hudson on any matter without the executive director's OK.

Today was a remarkable occasion at the Museum. Bernie Hudson wanted to meet with the entire staff, not just Frank Pruitt. And Cleo Walker had invited herself and asked Maria Sands to come, too. You were pleased that Hudson had called the meeting, but you were also glad that Cleo and Maria were there.

Bernie Hudson seemed primarily concerned about the upcoming capital campaign. "We have a big hill to climb, folks." Looking at Maria, Bernie blew a kiss. "I'll miss Maria by my side." Then he shrugged and started to continue.

Cleo Walker couldn't let the moment pass. "Bernie, we love you, but it's going to take more than your broad shoulders to carry us over the finish line."

"Of course, Cleo." Bernie looked flustered as she stepped on his lines. "I was getting to that." But Cleo was not about to back off, and after a few more jovial, but testy, exchanges between the founder and the board chair, Frank Pruitt hurriedly concluded the meeting. He looked at Sands, Walker,

Hudson, and you sitting awkwardly around the immense reception table.

"That was not nice, Cleo," Pruitt offered.

To Pruitt's surprise, Hudson did not get excited. Instead, he spoke quite calmly.

"I suppose, Cleo, that Maria's intention to resign has been difficult for you."

Cleo now spoke softly too. "Bernie, there are many ways to run an organization. Let me just say that this Museum has to find new ways of doing things around here."

Bernie scratched his head. "What a swell day this has turned out to be. So now what am I supposed to do?"

Cleo and Maria, almost in unison, wagged their fingers at their friend. "No, Bernie, what do we do? All of us."

What may very well distinguish you from others in an organization is a willingness to do your homework, so to speak, to sort out all of your observations and impressions so that you can shape a coherent picture of what the real organization looks like. To be an effective player early on does not necessarily mean being the first one out of the starting block. You are more likely to impress others by your preparation to run the race. People who do not do their detective work often act more precipitously and with negative results than those who ask more questions and "secure a solid base of information." There is "an inverse relationship between information gathering and readiness to act. The less information gathered, the greater the readiness to act. And vice versa."[9]

And the more you know, the more you realize how much there is to learn. Detective work is a state of mind. It is a readiness to question what someone else might readily accept or take for granted. It makes you a keener observer of the real organization, where culture, customs, and power relations reside, and prompts you to monitor these significant forces continuously. As they change over time, so does the real organization.

You will find in each succeeding chapter that a big part of organization smarts is to use your inquiring mind to find out what others think of you, to understand what others want, to know enough about what experts do and how they do it, and to identify organization problems early on before you are tempted to deny their existence. Your detective work really never ends.

CHAPTER 2

Establishing a Credible Reputation

It certainly matters what you can learn about a organization, and if you want to get ahead, it also matters what people in that organization learn about you. No one gets ahead without the help of others, and prospectors especially need to establish and maintain a credible reputation in all the networks and organizations they become part of.

Adam Smith noted: "'The success of . . . [most] people . . . almost always depends upon the favour and good opinion of their neighbors and equals; and without a tolerably regular conduct these can very seldom be obtained.'"[1] A good reputation is an especially invaluable asset for someone always ready to move on to new opportunities.

Organization smarts do not ensure a good reputation, but they make reputation building a first priority. And that is not so easy to do. Your performance, your character, even your prospects, are matters of opinion, aspects that are far from being within your control. What you think about your performance, your character, and your prospects does not necessarily dictate what others think about them. So reputation building is a curious joint venture. You own the project, but it's not yours alone to build.

First Impressions

In everyday life, you and I may encounter a host of strangers with no expectation of seeing them again, and if there were only one round in an organizational game, establishing a credible reputation would be of little consequence. There would be no "shadow of the future" to worry about. But in a multiround game, which corresponds to the numerous episodes that you share with other players in organizational life, they will look for some predictable characteristics of your play early on so that they can anticipate what you will do in succeeding rounds. When someone knows nothing about you, how you act in your first encounter can be a significant moment in shaping what your relationship will be. First impressions have consequences.

How you act then in the first round of an extended organizational game can set a precedent for the later rounds. If you are mindful of what is at stake, you can begin to establish your reputation. And when your style of play becomes consistent from one round to another and with one colleague after another, your reputation becomes credible.

To bring the idea of first impressions to life in a forum where people don't know each other yet, I ask them to pair up for what I call the "thumbs game." This is how the game is played.

THE THUMBS GAME:

1. The game consists of two players who pair up facing each other, making a fist with their right hands and then saying in unison "READY, SET . . . "

2. On "GO," a player shows either a THUMBS UP or a THUMBS DOWN.

3. The points awarded for each round of the game are as follows:

—If BOTH show THUMBS DOWN, they each get 1 POINT.

—If BOTH show THUMBS UP, they each get 3 POINTS.

—If player A shows a THUMBS DOWN and player B shows a THUMBS UP, player A gets 5 POINTS, and player B gets NO POINTS, or vice versa.

4. After playing ten rounds, participants are asked to characterize each other's play. Is the other player a "THUMBS-UPPER," a "THUMBS-DOWNER," or an "UNPREDICTABLE?" I put the characterization on a board next to the name of the player to whom it applies.

Everyone is asked to play the game with three different people. Before each ten rounds in a new pair, players look at the board to see how the play of the other person in their new pair has been characterized. The player with the most points after thirty rounds is the winner.

If I called it a "reputation game" in advance, then players would certainly be more mindful about the choices they make and the first impressions that others take away from the initial round of play. Calling it the thumbs game makes it a better learning device. Players don't have a chance to rehearse their performance. What I want them to do is look back and characterize each other's play so that when the game is finished they discover how important first impressions are in alerting others to how someone plays the game.

Such early impressions shape your reputation in an organization, and the making of your reputation depends not only on how you play the game but on how others interpret your play. There is as much room for misunderstanding as there is for clarification. It's what makes the thumbs game a useful approximation of what can happen in an organization with a host of different colleagues.

As part of the debriefing, I ask participants whether the characterizations of their play were accurate. Often they are not, but that underscores the risk as well as the opportunity in each encounter. For example, if you were a "thumbs-downer" in the very first round of play, it might be of little consequence to a player you were paired with who made the same choice. But if that player was committed to "thumbs-up" behavior regardless of the circumstances, your initial thumbs-down might make a lasting impression regardless of your behavior in later rounds. You would remain suspect to such a committed cooperator whose biased characterization of you would be passed on to others who might have nothing else to rely on.

Try playing the thumbs game with whomever you can find as a kind of rehearsal to discover or determine what your style of play is or should be. Do you prefer to be a "thumbs-upper," someone who always cooperates in a first encounter, or are you inclined to see a new encounter as a chance to gain some advantage?

If your rehearsal game shows that there is no particular pattern to your play, then your behavior may be characterized as "unpredictable," and your reputation in a multiround organizational game is likely to remain unsettled. Do you want to convey that impression in a new organizational setting? If people do not know what to expect from you, they may consider you unreliable or that your unpredictable behavior seems out of synch with the way others in the organization prefer to operate.

CITY HALL AND THE POLICE DEPARTMENT: This vignette illustrates how enmeshed you can become with precedents you inherit from your predecessors and how important it is to establish your own. As a newcomer, you may be suddenly confronted with choices of how to respond to the complaints, requests, and entreaties of those outside the immediate organization. They may be testing you to see just what kind of player you are. Their first impressions of you are important, too. They are familiar with how the game has been played and you are not. You may not know what you would do in the following vignette, but you should, at least, appreciate that each encounter is a reputation-making opportunity for you and for the mayor, as well.

When you agreed to work on the new mayor's staff, there had been no discussion of being a liaison between City Hall and the Police Department. It just seemed to work out that way during the first weeks of the new administration.

Perhaps the detectives who screen visitors in the City Hall rotunda sized you up and told their superiors that you were "friendly" or "important." They were veteran cops with a sixth sense about politics after pulling City Hall duty under three different administrations. They were part of the corridor gossip that livens up any desk job.

Perhaps events have just conspired to make you think about how much or how little City Hall should be involved in police matters, large or small. On the way to work this morning, you were still muddling over last night's phone call on your answering machine at home. The police lieutenant reported that a prominent legislator's car had been towed from a no-parking zone. The lieutenant told you that State Senator X was very angry and refused to pay. The officer had assured the senator that the car would be released if you gave the OK.

But events this morning did not offer you much time to muddle over last night's message. At 8 A.M. the new police commissioner called you.

"For the last six months, my guys have had a patrol car stationed in front of a synagogue on Eastern Drive twenty-four hours a day. It was put there after a number of anti-Semitic threats were made by phone and through the mails. My guys tell me that the former mayor put the cops there in the heat of his primary against your boss, and the threats are rather stale by now. But neighborhood leaders think 'all hell will break loose' if the car goes."

"Meaning what?" you mumbled.

The commissioner laughed. ""Meaning that the community likes the patrol car there, threats or no threats. Those folks will be on the mayor's doorstep before that car gets back to the station house. Hey, if City Hall wants the car there, it will stay."

You retreated to your office and started making a list of things to talk over with the mayor. You checked your calendar to see if the day had been officially designated "Police Day." There seemed little else on your immediate agenda.

Just before lunch, the president of the Patrolman's Benevolent Association called to complain that "some jerk" on the mayor's staff had drawn up new guidelines for who gets a parking permit in the City Hall lot.

"Guess what. I'm not on the charmed list anymore. Is that any way to treat a labor leader like yours truly? Well, is it?"

"I'll get back to you as soon as I can," you offered.

"Make it soon. I'm double-parked." He laughed and hung up.

Tit for Tat

You might want to consider a very simple strategy of play to establish a credible reputation in a new organization. It's called "tit for tat," which is to say, "do unto others as they do unto you." Not exactly a golden rule but a close relative of it. Think of it as a rule of thumb for the thumbs game.

Tit for tat asks you to shape a style of play that is both adaptive and consistent. At first blush, to be adaptive and to be consistent seem at odds, but they are not. The strategy of tit for tat has you reciprocate cooperation for cooperation (thumbs up) and noncooperation for noncooperation (thumbs down). You adapt to others while offering predictable responses. Such moves build a credible reputation quickly. You become known as someone who is always ready to cooperate but will not be played for a sucker.

Such adaptive behavior, however, does not tell you what to do in the initial round of your many two-person multiround games in the organization. Tit for tat would have you cooperate (thumbs up) in the first round using the golden rule. If your cooperation is not reciprocated in fair measure, then tit for tat has you reciprocate in kind (thumbs down) while remaining ready to return to a cooperative relationship if the other person gets the message and resumes cooperating in your next round together. After the first round, you become known as someone who is a *conditional* thumbs-upper.

At first glance, tit for tat does not seem to have a mind of its own, but that is not really true. You develop a credible reputation for initiating cooperation but make it clear that you are not willing to let others take advantage of you. The simple progression of play for your tit for tat strategy is (1) cooperate in the first round with your thumbs up; (2) continue to cooperate in succeeding rounds as long as the other person cooperates with a thumbs up; (3) be prepared to terminate cooperation immediately with a thumbs down if that person defects with a thumbs down; but (4) don't hold a grudge if the person resumes cooperation with a thumbs up and reciprocate immediately with your own thumbs up.[2]

Adapting your play to others and the consistency with which you do it clarify how you treat others and how you want to be treated. When others find that there is nothing unpredictable about you, you will have fewer adjustments to make. As those who have not yet played the game with you learn about your style of play, they are likely to adapt their play to yours. Why? In the thumbs game, two thumbs-downers collect fewer points than two thumbs-uppers who sustain their cooperation through ten rounds. In a multiround game, consistent cooperation is more productive than the short-term gain of defection in any particular round.

When people are leaving an organization, they may be less interested in sustaining cooperative relationships and will just pursue their narrow self-interests. They no longer see themselves in a multiround game, their heads are out the door, and the interests of the organization and their colleagues become secondary. But to abandon tit for tat in the last round of an organizational game can be counterproductive. Your organizational exits can be as important as your organizational entrances. Last impressions, just like first impressions, have consequence, something that I discuss below in "Living up to your reputation."

Tit for tat is not a "winner's" strategy, but it is a way to establish a credible reputation as someone who is ready to contribute to the welfare of colleagues as long as they return the favor. That's not a bad way to introduce yourself to a new organization when people are trying to size you up. It's also not a bad way to be remembered when you leave.

Furthermore, as a prospector you probably remain networked with a lot of people who may have little to do with your latest organization hitch or assignment. They are your former colleagues from other organizations, your friends, mentors, contacts—a host of pairings where tit for tat also gets played out. Your reputation with them may have already been established, but to maintain or enhance it, returning favor for favor or declining to do so when someone has let you down, makes sense in your network relations.

A great deal is written these days about "reciprocity" and "trust" as the essential lubricants of networking. Tit for tat is the game of choice in such circumstances and a good strategy for reputation building both inside an organization and with the web of connections that any prospector needs to move on and get ahead.

> **THE ENVELOPE GAME:** You will find that tit for tat does not clarify when to cooperate in large undertakings, in which your specific contribution may go unnoticed. Your reputation in a multiperson game is of less consequence. To illustrate, I use what I call the "envelope game" to let people experience why cooperative behavior is far more likely to arise between two persons or in small groups than in large undifferentiated ones.[3]

I hand out an empty envelope to each participant, usually twenty-five or more, and tell them that it represents both an opportunity and a risk.

"You can put any amount of money, or none at all, in your envelope. All envelopes will be returned to me. If the total amount of money in all the envelopes is more than $75 (assuming there are twenty-five players), you will each get $5. If the total is less than $75, you will each get nothing, and I will donate the money to my favorite charity."

No communication is permitted among the players in this game, and they are not allowed to show anyone what they put in their respective envelopes. The players are given ten minutes to choose what to do and return their envelopes to me. All of this is done anonymously. When I open each envelope, no one knows whose it is.

In the many times that I have played the envelope game, I have lost only once. Why is it that I don't have to part with my money? When the one-round multiperson game is analyzed, the dominant strategy is to "defect," that is, put nothing in your envelope. You risk losing no money, and you have the opportunity of getting some for yourself if others put enough money in their envelopes to meet the target amount of $75.01. The dilemma is, however, that if everyone else pursues such a strategy, the target amount will not be met and no one will gain. The choice to defect, then, is not the choice you want others to make.

Even if you shun the strategy of a free rider, you may hesitate to contribute your fair share ($3) because you fear that others will not contribute theirs. If others have the same fear, the collective effort will fail. Some will put no money in their envelopes or less than their fair share because they are skeptical about the prospects of success.

Those who are willing to do more than their fair share not only incur a greater cost but run the risk that their contribution will not make enough difference. Those whose resources, altruism, or leadership are put to work in a collective effort usually welcome the opportunity, but they also assume the risk that the enterprise may fail despite their contributions.

Barring communication in the game mirrors the difficulty of collective action when a relatively large number of people are not in direct contact and do not have adequate information about each other.

I have already noted that organizational life is not a one-round game like the envelope game, but it can pose some of the same problems, which is why cooperation is more likely when smaller working groups are formed. The risks of the envelope game are mitigated by open communication and each person's contribution makes a greater difference. There is more pressure for everyone to do his or her fair share, and it is easier to monitor cooperation and devise sanctions, if necessary.

The Company You Keep

The thumbs game makes clear that there is no objective truth about anyone's reputation. Some of it is shaped by whom you play with, not just how you play. If an organization is full of "thumbs-uppers," your style of play is measured against their preferred style. In fact, your reputation may be subsumed by the organization's reputation. To underscore this point, at the conclusion of the thumbs game, I ask the participants whether they would be interested in being associated with the winner—the person who had the highest number of points for the thirty rounds played—and the organization in which that person works. Such an organization might very well have a reputation, a culture, very similar to the winner's style of play. Whatever that style is, the participants are likely to be divided in their responses. "Thumbs-uppers" prefer a cooperative culture; "thumbs-downers" prefer an organization that encourages competition.

As a prospector, when you associate with a particular organization, your reputation is likely to be affected by how outsiders perceive what is valued at that place. They adjust their play to account for those values as well as for the style of play you bring to your multiround games with them. The adage "people are known by the company they keep" carries some weight. Similarly, your individual reputation can be shaped by the reputation (the subculture) of a particular division or department in an organization with which you are identified. When moving on to a new workplace, it makes sense to learn as much as you can about what outsiders think of that organization and what insiders think of the unit where you do most of your work. Their opinions may prove to be shallow, but even stereotypical thinking can add to or detract from your individual standing. Like it or not, an organization's culture and any subculture you become part of do make a difference in what people think of you.

What if the reputation that you want to establish does not fit with how a unit of the organization itself is already known? For example, if you thrive on competition in a place that does not value such an attitude, you may have to make some adjustments. The people with whom you work influence how you are perceived by those more distant in the organization. Your "fit' with them may affect what they say about you to others. Of course, you may want to move on if it is self-defeating to fit in where you prefer to stand out.

In large organizations, most people will not have a chance to know you well. They will base their perceptions on indirect evidence, your title, your unit, and, among other clues, the opinions of those who work directly with you. Inquiries about your reputation are a shortcut for people who do not have the opportunity or access to find out for themselves. For better or worse, your reputation is brokered by those who know you best.

I remember having my reputation in City Hall brokered by members of my staff. Their opinions about me were often solicited by relative strangers, and they also reported back on what others were saying about me. It provided me with important feedback about my reputation. I learned that people thought I had enormous influence with the mayor, which was not entirely true. However, as long as that was the perception, my power to influence the mayor was enhanced because I became the conduit that others used, thinking that their interests would get a hearing.

How you become known in a large organization should be important to you. For example, being part of a network or group gives you the opportunity to become known for predictable behavior—as an initiator of new ideas, as a source of reliable information, or as someone who always solicits others' opinions or who tries to mediate conflicts that arise. The word gets around about you, and players you have not even met may come to think of you in a certain way.

It is not easy, however, to always account for what "they" will say about you, especially when you are a newcomer. Grapevines in an organization trade on gossip and rumor serving as channels for speculative and highly partisan opinions. You may not have access to these grapevines to know what "they" are saying. If you can find someone who can tell you, it is important feedback, accurate or inaccurate, about yourself. You have little control over what is being said, but it may tell you what you should be doing to correct any wrong impressions.

"I've heard good things about you" is what you want to hear from someone in a large organization when you find yourself working with him for the first time. You certainly won't disagree with the compliment, but you may wonder how he learned about you. Who talks to whom and how the word about you gets around is impossible to trace. All you can really know from such a comment is that so far the way you have conducted yourself with others has made a good impression and been reinforced as it gets passed along.

No one is likely to say, "I've heard bad things about you." When the news is negative, you rarely get firsthand feedback. Bad reputations once established in large organizations are hard to change, just like the difficulty in reconstructing your creditworthiness if a credit bureau keeps telling others of your past transgressions. Consider the example of a new higher-up who misuses the power of his position to further his own personal interests. He may have formal authority in the organization, but his conduct probably robs him of the influence he needs to get people working with him productively. He has to earn such working authority; it is not conferred simply by having a big title, office, and staff.

Organizations have more resources to rehabilitate their good name than you do. They use public relations and advertising to change or improve their corporate image, but if you are in a large organization, you have to win over opinion one colleague at a time until enough colleagues tell enough others of your makeover. Your reputation is eventually remade, but it takes a great deal of time and effort, more time than you probably have as a prospector. And what makes it worse is that a bad reputation can dog you wherever you head next. Some people who move on are immediately suspect if they are seen as trying to stay one step ahead of the reputation they would prefer to leave behind. All the more reason to create positive first impressions of yourself in a large organization, before you lose control of your reputation or lose touch with those who help shape it.

TAXPRO, INC.: Sometimes an organization becomes seriously divided, and your reputation may hinge on whose side people think you are on.

A critical date for the management of TaxPro, Inc., is next Tuesday. That is the day that a delegation of institutional investors, which hold 65 percent of the company's stock, is expecting some kind of reorganization plan to stem the fall in profits. The institutional investors have become skittish about the earning prospects of TaxPro and want to know why they should retain the company's stock in their portfolios.

TaxPro's founder and continuing chairman of the board is Fred Blomberg, who built a national company of income tax preparers from two offices originating in Memphis, Tennessee. Over the years, TaxPro captured almost 20 percent of the tax preparation business. As the company grew, it acquired MacroLink, whose core business has been point-of-sale credit card authorization servers and, more recently, electronic mail, database access, and Internet-related services. As TaxPro's business has stagnated with the advent of more simplified tax forms and more competition from national accounting firms, MacroLink's earnings have exceeded TaxPro's as a percentage of the total combined business.

Recently, A. Peter Samuelson, the vice president in charge of MacroLink, was asked by the outside directors on

TaxPro's board to take over the presidential duties of Fred Blomberg, making "old Fred" the chair and CEO, which they considered a less stressful position for the company's founder. In recent years, Blomberg has been spending more time in Florida, believing his decentralized style of management would work quite well, even in his absence. Such a corporate suite change has alarmed many of the managers at TaxPro, who saw Fred Blomberg as a much gentler and more easygoing executive than Samuelson, who favored tight fiscal and service development controls when he managed MacroLink.

You are a relatively new executive to the TaxPro side of the business, but a favorite of Fred Blomberg, and Samuelson has asked for your help on a reorganization plan. At the same time, Blomberg has urged you to support the promotion and reward of talented women managers on the TaxPro side of the business as part of any reorganization plan. He is concerned that if Samuelson centralizes the organization again, the decentralized style that encouraged managers, mainly women, to take the initiative in service development and improvement will be out of favor.

One issue in any reorganization plan that emerges is what TaxPro will do with its electronic filing software unit, which is headed by a woman. At one time the unit had been at the center of Blomberg's plans to serve the increasing percentage of taxpayers who wanted to file their tax returns electronically, but the earnings have been very disappointing. Blomberg sees her as a very bright manager of technical people, giving them wide scope in design and implementation, but her management style is almost the direct opposite of Samuelson's.

Blomberg is also worried about the fate of the nation-wide network of TaxPro training schools and the woman who manages that piece of the business. The schools were a part of Fred's original vision, but in recent years they have become more costly to maintain, as fewer local C.P.A.'s attended them or signed up with national accounting firms competing to get a greater share of the tax preparation market. Blomberg does not think, however, that the woman who oversees the schools should be blamed for market forces beyond her control but suspects that Samuelson sees no "synergy" of the training schools with MacroLink, which has fast become the core business of the organization.

It seems that all of the corporate units headed by women hired by Fred Blomberg are in jeopardy, given the pressures to satisfy the institutional investors from those now trying to take charge on the top executive floor. How do you establish your reputation when loyalties are so divided?

Walking Your Talk

One way to establish a credible reputation in a new organization is to make your actions consistent with your words. Whatever assurances you give or deadlines you set, be sure you can walk your talk. If you become known as someone who does, it helps you immeasurably in the bargaining games of organizational life.

I use the term "bargaining" loosely here to describe encounters when you want to persuade others that your position on a matter is thoughtful, not capricious, and that they can expect that you will follow through with actions that are consistent with your position. You want your "talk" to be believable, or people will not be inclined to take you seriously. Will you actually do what you say? It matters a great deal to your reputation.[4]

Let me give you an illustration of the subtle bargaining that goes on all the time in an organization. Imagine that you are trying to get a RFP (request for proposal) out the door and your new colleagues are tardy in providing feedback to a draft that you have circulated. So you alert them by e-mail: "If I don't hear from you by Thursday with suggestions on how we can improve my draft RFP, I will send it out for publication on Friday to start the bidding process. We can't afford to fall behind in the project schedule."

You are telling your colleagues that you want their input, but you can't afford to wait any longer. You have established a deadline that serves to end one phase of the project and to begin another. When you limit your options or course of action, you limit what others can do as well. Your Thursday deadline forces your colleagues to focus on what you want from them or forego the opportunity to revise your draft.

Your deadline is credible if the reasons for it are credible. There is nothing in your e-mail that is not true. It is always easier to persuade others of what is true than of what you know or they may think is a bluff or just posturing on your part. You don't want your judgment and word to become suspect. Think back to the mid-nineties, when Congressional Republicans declared that they would let the federal government default on its bonds redeemable on a certain date unless their proposed federal budget was approved by the Clinton administration. Apparently, the Republicans' threat to shut down the government was not believable to the White House, and the Republicans soon backed down.

Your talk may be less momentous than a Capitol Hill showdown, but if it does not seem plausible to others under a given set of organizational circumstances, then it will be difficult for you to follow through. And when that happens, people may take whatever you say less seriously in the future. Once your word is doubted, you will find it harder to get things done that require not just your follow-through but the cooperation of others as well.

Assuming you do in fact go ahead and send out the RFP for publication on Friday, your colleagues quickly learn that you follow through after whatever deadlines you set. The next time it will be easier for you to get their input when you want it. Making the simple case that a deadline is reasonable, given the surrounding circumstances, makes their timely compliance more likely. Even if some of your deadlines become arbitrary, your colleagues may very well comply because of your reputation for making good on what you say.

Deadline or not, you don't want to be thought of as a person who has to say something three times to convince others that you really want action. Walking your talk consistently should avoid that. Otherwise, like the boy who cried wolf when there was no wolf, you put yourself at risk when there is an urgent situation but no one believes you anymore. Have you ever worked with someone, as I have, who often seems to forget entirely what he asked you to do? At first my reaction is to be responsive, but when I learn that he takes less seriously his own request than I did, I begin to doubt the necessity to be so responsive. I may wait until he asks me again or even a third time. I don't want to walk his talk unless he means it.

What do you do when you just don't want to walk someone else's talk regardless of whether he means it or not? You may be able to persuade him that your hands are tied, that you are not free to do what he wants you to do. For example, assume that he asks for your help in implementing a proposal that you think is seriously flawed. Rather than criticizing your colleague's proposal directly, you tell him: "I know my boss won't agree to that. Why don't you make certain revisions that will make it more acceptable to her?" In this instance, you act as an agent for your boss, which may convince your colleague to make the revisions because you have made clear that ultimate approval is out of your hands. Of course, you should be confident that your reading of a higher-up is accurate. Much the same is done when a union leader declares that his membership will never accept a particular wage package offered, or a negotiator for management declares that her hands are tied because her board will not permit her to offer a more generous settlement.

There are many occasions when, for the sake of maintaining good working relations, you may want, in the best sense, to hide behind others: "My boss would never let me do this," or "I know my staff can't go along with that." You may also want to seek other kinds of shelter: "The rules won't allow me to do what you want," or "If I did it for you, in fairness I would have to do it for everyone else."

In each instance, however, you should not invoke higher-ups or rules or standards of fairness if you are using them only as excuses. Your logic, not your resistance, should be what impresses those you seek to persuade. And if you are consistent and use the same logic on subsequent occasions, you are likely to find that people start accepting rather than constantly testing your way of handling certain matters. And that certainly makes it easier for you; your reputation becomes more credible.

Rules in particular are often invoked without further discussion. This can gall people who may be forced to accept a rule but bridle at its existence. You can help them understand why you can't act on their behalf or provide them with what they want, by discussing why a rule exists and should be followed. Rules are a shelter, but they should not be just a door slammed in someone's face. Look for the reason for a rule and take the time to explain it. It is likely to make both you and the rule more credible to those affected by it.

Some people use rules in organizations in part to avoid personal accountability. The rule makes them do what they do. More persuasive, however, is when you remain accountable to others despite a rule by taking the time to walk them through your talk.

THE LIFE OF A STATE INVESTIGATION COMMISSION:

I once was chair of a temporary bipartisan state investigation commission. My position was full time, and there were three other commissioners who served in a part-time capacity. The statutory life of the commission had to be renewed by the legislature every two years. The commission had been in existence for nineteen years and employed forty investigators, auditors, lawyers, and administrative staff.

On the eve of another two-year extension of the commission's life by the state senate, I received a phone call at 10 P.M., two hours before the senate had to act either to renew the life of the temporary commission or let it expire. It was the top aide of the Republican majority leader of the state senate who informed me in no uncertain terms that no action would be taken to extend the commission's life unless I agreed to rehire the commission's chief investigator, whom I had fired recently for unsatisfactory performance. What was I to do?

It is very easy for a bystander to say: "What an outrageous demand. Politics as usual. Don't give in, David, or you'll be no better than they are." But I also had to consider what I would say the next morning to forty employees who would have been out of a job, not to mention yours truly.

With only two hours before the commission might turn into a pumpkin, my mind had to get into high gear. I told the aide I would call him back within the hour. I had been given a deadline by an agent for his higher-up, the senate majority leader. They were tightening the screws on me.

If I had thought the phone call was no more than a last-minute bluff, I could have refused their demand and waited for them to back down. Was the deadline threat credible, believable? I thought it was. I had heard that they had played this game at other times and with great success. Could I speak directly to the majority leader? Not likely. His unavailability made it impossible for me to negotiate with the source of the demand.

What could I do to overcome my disadvantage? Should I tell the majority leader's aide that I was unable to reach my fellow commissioners and therefore could not respond? Two can play the "agent" game, but what if they could, in fact, reach my commissioners when I had said that I could not?

I knew for sure there was at least one commissioner who should know what was going on, my Republican colleague on the commission. Could he dissuade his party's majority leader in the senate? Not likely, but if we stood together, any response we made would be more credible. I decided that the better course of action was to threaten a press conference the next morning detailing why the commission's life had been terminated, provided that my Republican commissioner was willing to stand with me. To his credit, he agreed that he would *if* that were necessary.

Would my brinkmanship be believable to the senate majority leader? I thought so, since I had already established a nonpartisan reputation, free of patronage, in overseeing the affairs of the commission. Would he back off before midnight? I thought so, because it would be much easier to do

> so in our private give-and-take than for him to risk a public
> backlash the next day.
>
> My Republican colleague on the commission called the
> majority leader's aide and told him of our intentions. Their
> phone call ended abruptly. The next morning my assistant
> confirmed that the state senate had renewed the life of the
> commission for another two years. I smiled: "Oh, that is rou-
> tine business for those guys. Just another day at the office."

Living Up to Your Reputation

As you move on from one organization to another, assuming that
you are getting ahead and not just on the run, you no doubt
acquire a reputation for effort, performance, being a team player,
and so forth, that makes people want to make room for you in their
organizations.

But this is where it can get tricky. In hiring circles you become a
known quantity, but you also have to adapt your performance to the
particular culture, customs, and power relations of any organization
that you encounter. Everything that I have discussed in this chapter—first impressions, tit for tat, the company you keep, and walking your talk—is tested in new circumstances, and your reputation,
which preceded you, only becomes credible when you live up to it.

Living up to your reputation is fulfilling other people's expectations. See it as a good thing. It should keep you on your toes and
make you work that much harder to earn the respect of your new
colleagues. Besides, there will be many others who are either totally
ignorant or out of the loop about who you are and what you bring.
So you have to impress not only those who think they know
enough about you to bring you into their enterprise but those
already there who don't have a clue about you.

It helps to know why you were hired or contracted for in the first place. You may think you know based on your own self-assessment and assuming that you have been the architect of the reputation you bring to a new organization. But what you think of yourself and what you've done does not always explain what others see in you and why they want your services. Your own estimate of your reputation is not enough. In the search process or when you first arrive, you should make an effort to clarify what it is about you that others particularly value. It may not be so obvious as you think. And if you don't know why you were chosen, you may find it harder to fulfill their expectations.

Anyone in the position of choosing talented people knows a great deal more than the candidates do about what kind of people a unit or organization needs, given its current state. Those who size you up use measures of your fit for specific organizational problems and undertakings that you probably can know little about at the outset. Why were you chosen? Those in charge may not tell you unless you ask. Can you learn something about your reputation that you didn't know or were not sure of? Getting such feedback makes it easier to live up to your reputation, knowing what it looks like from someone's point of view other than your own.

REFERENCES: When moving on, choose your references carefully. References are a triangulation of opinion, which serve as a temporary shorthand for the reputation you would like to project. References should say more than "I know Joe Blow and recommend him to you." Good references usually include some discussion about reputation, although that word may not be used. "Among his peers, Joe Blow is known for his cooperative attitude, and his consistent record of follow-through with whatever job he has to do, and his team spirit is appreciated by everyone he works with." Look for people who can speak for others, not just themselves. If your reputation is a good one, find those who are representative of the general opinion about you, not just isolated friends whose viewpoints may be discounted.

When I look at someone's references, I know they will be generally positive. Why would anyone offer any other kind of reference? Can you imagine a producer of a Broadway show trying to sell tickets after running an ad that quotes reviewers who say, "A ho-hum show" or "Don't bother"? I find references are useful when they reinforce each other. If three letters of reference or my conversations with references all highlight the same attributes, they become more credible to me.

Too many times, however, I sense that references do not accurately portray the person that I am considering. Wouldn't it be nice, as it once was in ancient China, if recommenders could be held accountable for the people they recommend? But that is not the case, so I seek out other sources of opinion who become my references, not the applicant's. Applicants use their discretion in determining who will speak for them. I understand that. What I want are references who are willing to help me and not necessarily the applicant. Where do I find such people?

First, whom does the applicant not include that common sense tells me should be included—a former employer, a faculty adviser, someone who is prominent in the circles in which the applicant moves?

Second, whom do I know who knows the applicant? Such references are far more valuable to me because there is an existing or prior relationship between us. When I act as a reference, I am more careful in my recommendations to those I know than to those I don't. I owe the former a little more. After all, they may reciprocate in kind when it is their turn to help me evaluate a stranger at my door.

Third, I look for people who know the applicant *and* who are familiar with my organization. Such people can help me evaluate the fit. Of course, I can describe my organization in the course of asking people about the applicant, but if they are able to rely on their own impressions of the organization and not just on mine, they are likely to be more discerning in matching the applicant to the opportunity.

Even with such detective work, it is very dicey hiring strangers. My batting average is about .500. I wish it were better. I don't blame the references who misled me. I should know that they stand with the applicant, not me. And sometimes there has not been sufficient time to pin down a stranger's reputation with a friend of mine who owed more to the applicant than to me. Like a Broadway opening, there may be mixed reviews, and even if you read them all, you don't know what to make of a production, or an applicant. As they say, "You pays your money and you takes your chance," and sometimes you are delighted with what you see and sometimes you wonder why on earth you could be so wrong, or why the reviewers were.

For most of this chapter, I have looked at your reputation in the making as one that begins at the front door when you enter an organization, when you play their multiround game, and how they interpret your play and what they say about it to others. But I have also noted that opinions about you follow you from job to job, from organization to organization, so that your reputation in any particular place is just one chapter of a longer story that you write yourself but that others rework based on their reading of you.

Therefore, in contemplating a move to a new organization, don't just think about who will be your references. Consider that your reputation may turn on what any colleague says about you and that you want to anticipate such opinion *before* you decide to move on. What can you do to win over or win back those who have been critical of your performance? When people get ready to make a move, they often forget that their exits are remembered as well as their entrances. They are too busy looking ahead—"I'm outta here"—to review their current status in an organization and whose good opinion they will need to get ahead, wherever they choose to go.

Since you rarely know what someone will say about you after you leave an organization, there is a lot to gain in thinking carefully about how you orchestrate your departure and the reasons you give for leaving. Both may be important to your ex-colleagues who are asked about you at some later date. You may not ask them to serve as references, but their opinions, nonetheless, may reach those whom you need to get ahead. Like "six degrees of separation," the distance between so-called strangers is less than we think—someone there knows someone here and the word about you gets out, gets around through acquaintances and networks that neither you nor anyone else can imagine or control.

CHAPTER 3

Understanding What Others Want

At the heart of successful prospecting is the challenge to understand what others want. This may seem curious for those who prospect from job to job and organization to organization, caught up with self-advancement and gaining a competitive edge. But looking out for number one is bound up in learning how to work with your colleagues of the moment. Independence and interdependence are not mutually exclusive. After all, the real organization is more theirs than yours, and your reputation is in their hands, not just your own. You're not going to get very far without them.

A prospector lacks the experience and status that veterans in an organization have acquired. Veterans are very different. They have stayed put in a place they know well. They don't want to start over someplace else with the effort and risk that such change entails. Their performance has improved with repetitive tasks and their familiarity with one another. In fact, the organization would not work very well if it were only staffed with prospectors. So you cannot afford to distance yourself from them, assert your preferences, and expect to get much done. Any preference by definition acknowledges that what others want matters, too.

Your preferences, like your prospects, are what center you, but they are better realized when you can get out of yourself and shift the center, temporarily at least, to the other guy. There is even a word for it, "allocentric," in *Webster's Third New International Dictionary,* which means to have "one's interest and attention centered on other persons."[1] So in this chapter we take up the art of putting yourself in the other person's shoes and the importance of setting aside your normal wardrobe, who you are and what you have acquired, for the wardrobe of those you know less well. It's not done to show that you care about them or to be empathetic, as important as that may be. You do it primarily to reconcile your preferences with those of your colleagues. It is hard and never-ending work driven by the grudging recognition that problem solving in organizations is an unavoidable enterprise shared by interdependent players.

Putting yourself in the other person's shoes is also a necessary preliminary for thinking strategically. To think strategically does not mean devising a game plan, which is often associated with "strategy." A game plan is a projection of what someone wants to happen, but it is much easier to construct the plan than to play the game. Thinking strategically is the ability to anticipate, influence, and adjust to the preferences of the other players. Understanding what others want is critical to every round you play. Let's see how it works when framing problems with others, working with higher-ups, preparing for meetings, getting the commitment of others, and voting or bargaining with them.

Framing Problems with Others

Many of the problems that you confront in your daily life outside work are yours to deal with alone. Framing a problem helps you organize an uncertain situation: "I'm spending more each month than I'm earning, and the cost of borrowing is making the gap more difficult to close." Then you look for a solution or, at least, for another credit card to consolidate your debt at a lower interest rate.

When you confront a problematic situation in an organization, however, you are not on your own, even though your habits and training may prompt you to think and act without reference to others. You are prone to what I would call "sincere behavior."

Sincere behavior operates from the laudable premise that others in an organization are entitled to an honest rendering of what you value and what you believe, the expression of your unique and authentic self. "This is the way I feel about X. I just don't think it's right . . ."

Sincere behavior also includes your making competent use of the specialized skills for which you were hired or retained in the first place. "The best way to look at Y is to do a cost-benefit analysis . . ."

And merely saying "If I were you" is not enough. Such advice is more a polite way of advancing your own opinion than trying to see the matter from a different point of view. That's not putting yourself in the other person's shoes; that's putting him in yours—a big difference. Assuming that you think well of yourself and of your skills, your sincere behavior makes you understandably self-centered, relying on your values and training to shape how you look at an organization's problems. It is natural and in most respects healthy for individuals in an organization to assert their unique identities and specialized roles. But sincere behavior is as much a liability as it is an asset. The values that you profess or the methods that you want to use are not likely to be accepted without reservation by your colleagues.

Someone is likely to say: "You're entitled to your opinion, but what about Joe's seniority in the matter, and have you considered how a woman like Angela might feel?"

Somebody else points out: "You always want to do a cost-benefit analysis, but Jane wants to try a focus group and Miguel's gut instinct tells him . . ."

Your colleagues remind you that there are many other values and methods to consider other than your own. In organizational life, strategic behavior, taking into account others' preferences and acting with those preferences in mind, is equally important. It makes a difference how Joe, Angela, Jane, and Miguel are likely to frame a problem.

When individuals stand at different places in a mountain valley, their estimates about which is the highest peak are bound to differ. Similarly, when people stand in different places in an organization, they are likely to have different perspectives about what the problem is. Framing a problem is an act of choosing. Just like you, your colleagues' choice of a problem frame usually depends on their specialized training, organizational role, or personal values. It is not enough to think you know what the problem is. It also matters what the other players think the problem is. It is not enough to think you know what the solution is. It also matters if the other players think that your solution fits their conception of what the problem is. And even if your solution does, it is possible that they may think they have better solutions than yours. Your "right answer" or your "right values" don't necessarily win the day in organizational life, where answers and values are contested.[2]

When you frame a problem with others, getting it right is often less important than getting agreement on how to proceed. The problem frame is not "out there" in some territory to be discovered by your preferred method or "in here" where your personal beliefs reside. The likely problem frame usually lies between and among all of you and has to be constructed together. There will be no highest peak that can be measured that confirms the perspective of one of you and rejects the perspectives of everyone else. More likely your search will be for a workable consensus. Why? Because there is little chance that once a problem is framed that you or anyone else, higher up or lower down, can solve it alone. When we frame a problem with others, we are hoping to get a buy-in from those we need to resolve it. "Owning" a problem does not guarantee that it will be resolved successfully, but those who take part in the framing process are likely to share more willingly in the follow-through.

CITY ELECTRIC: In the following vignette, how would you frame the problem facing City Electric? Will Pat McCoy agree with you? Janet Freeman? Vernon Backus?

When you were retained recently as an interim manager of the human resources department at City Electric, you quickly learned how much trouble the public utility was in. CE serves one million customers in a tristate area, but it has fallen, at least temporarily, on hard times. Fearful a decade ago that it would not have enough reserve generating capacity to serve its projected customer base, it launched an ambitious expansion and modernization program. Unfortunately, growth of the customer base did not materialize as planned, and profits have been disappointing.

Pat McCoy, CE's CEO, knows that layoffs will be difficult, given its aggressive affirmative action hiring policies of recent years. Under political pressure and with the help of outside consultants, CE's management came to realize that its workforce was not representative of its customer service area. With urging from her board of directors, McCoy hired Janet Freeman to develop a "balanced workforce plan."

Freeman, a longtime resident of the service area and active in civil rights and community affairs, produced a plan for CE that included moving minorities up faster into managerial ranks, tracking minority representation by operating unit, and providing career support. But central to the plan was increasing the percentage of minorities in the construction division. Most employees in that division have been unskilled and worked as cement finishers. Freeman saw to it that a skills program, where employees could learn building trades other than their own, was incorporated. The program is still too young to produce what one wag called "concrete results."

The "balanced workforce plan" at CE has not been welcomed with open arms by company veterans. Vernon Backus, the vice president for quality control, has privately questioned the speed with which Freeman and top management implemented the plan. Backus nonetheless has been a team player and is a believer in affirmative action as long as such a policy does not undermine his wing of the business, which means "doing projects right, on time, and within budget."

Backus knows that any downsizing in CE's construction division presents tough choices. Newly hired minority workers appear to be the most vulnerable if senior workers are to be retained to keep construction quality where the company wants it. Experience and seniority remain essentially the preserve of a white male cadre in the construction division, and such employees will not look kindly on being laid off in order to favor less experienced workers.

Pat McCoy has another concern. Yesterday, Belinda Armstrong, a savvy investment banker who has tracked CE's fortunes over the years, brought some merger speculation to McCoy's attention.

"There is a possibility, Pat, that MidAtlantic CoGeneration, seeing your company's distress, might like to make CE part of its regional delivery infrastructure. They are bigger and have deeper pockets than you and can absorb your operations and workforce without a blink."

"Bee, I would hate to have CE get swallowed by a company that is known for imposing its play-to-win culture on everything it touches. All they care about is rewarding those who bring in the most business. Besides, our employee relations are in enough jeopardy now with the prospect of downsizing."

"I understand, Pat, but do consider that MidAtlantic's bid might avoid big layoffs if your financials get tucked into that giant's consolidated statements. Hey, I know you don't want to lose control. You're too young to be turned out to pasture, but maybe MidAtlantic will keep you and your team on instead of bringing in their own troops."

At a staff meeting this morning, to which Belinda Armstrong was invited, Janet Freeman showed no fear of McCoy or anyone else. "What bothers me, Pat, is that our 'balanced workforce plan' has not been given enough time to show truly positive results."

Vernon Backus was quick with a rejoinder: "You know I support your efforts, Janet, but my people have been pushed to implement these time-consuming programs, and something had to give. I'm afraid it was productivity, and our construction costs show it."

Before Freeman could respond, Belinda Armstrong decided to intervene. "If CE's major stockholders don't like the return on their investment, they may soon have two choices. Sell and put the company's stock price into a free fall or sell out to MidAtlantic CoGeneration, which may seek a takeover of CE."

Vernon Backus couldn't sit still. "Janet," as he walked away from the table, "everyone's job in this room would be up for grabs. But more important, MidAtlantic plays hardball, and if they don't like our bottom line, they just might put our 'balanced workforce plan' in mothballs so fast it would make your head spin."

At that moment, CE's VP for external affairs rushed in with a report telling of a meeting between MidAtlantic's CEO and a delegation of CE's institutional investors. A spokesperson for the delegation gave CE's management "one week to get its act together."

Working with Higher-Ups

When you figure out the power relations in an organization, it certainly includes your own working relationships, and none is more central than you and your boss. Everybody is a lower-down to some higher-up. In fact, you may have quite a few higher-ups to keep track of, but there is probably one higher-up whom you consider the boss. As a newcomer and lower-down, however, you are not as much at a disadvantage as you might think.

It's fair to assume that the boss is probably in over his head. In an era when higher-ups, like everyone else, come and go with bewildering regularity, many of them are installed or promoted without adequate training or experience, and they are running scared like everyone else. Your boss may bluff that he knows what he is doing, but, like a swimmer far from shore and over his head, he probably needs lots of help. A boss is undoubtedly the key to critical information and more resources, and he has the upper hand when it comes to hiring, evaluation, and promotion. But such authority obscures a mutual dependence, and understanding his preferences is the place to start in making the relationship work to your mutual advantage.

First, analyze your strengths and weaknesses in relation to his. Some higher-ups prefer to hire those who are like themselves. Such compatibility promotes a good working relationship, but if your strengths and weaknesses mirror his, that may work to your mutual disadvantage. For example, you may share similar backgrounds that make both of you insensitive to colleagues who are not like you, or you may both prefer to do detail work with little interest or talent for the necessary hand-holding of those who need support and encouragement. What can you do to help him make some adjustments? If you are not like him, your strengths may compensate for his weaknesses. It will certainly make it more likely that he will give you important work for which he is not suited. If he sees you as an indispensable player and not just a lower-down waiting for leftovers from his agenda, delegation is a lot easier. I say more about this in the next section under "Who does what."

Second, ask yourself whether you are the kind of person who is overdependent on those in authority or counterdependent, someone who resists authority.[3] Work relationships with higher-ups and lower-downs may not be that far removed from family history. I certainly put myself in the counterdependent category. It has something to do with having an older brother who was always in charge of our childhood games. I love him dearly, but I spent a part of my life getting out of his shadow with no desire to put myself in someone else's. For some other younger brother that shadow might be a secure place to be reestablished with a higher-up. In any event, you should understand what your preference is and how it may hinder the development of a good working relationship with your boss. If you have a number of misunderstandings with him, try asking others whether they have experienced the same problem. If they have not, the reason for the misunderstandings may be a mismatch of expectations in your relationship. He may be a hostage of his family history, too.

Third, the work habits that you bring to a job or have developed with previous higher-ups may or may not fit the operating style of a new boss. Start by putting yourself in his shoes. How does he prefer to communicate on important matters—by e-mail, phone, one-on-one, staff meetings? I used to tell my staff that I preferred to have short conversations to discuss ongoing business. "If you want to make a record of the matter, send me your memo. If you want to get something done, let's talk." I wanted the give-and-take of a conversation, not the monologue of a lengthy memo. Some people hide behind their e-mails, even when you're in the office next door or just down the hall. If, however, I thought that a staff member's comments in a face-to-face meeting seemed tentative or confused, I might ask for something in writing. It was a plea for clarity. "Please tell me what you're trying to say." Every higher-up prefers communicating in a certain way, and part of your initial adjustment is to make sure you match your communication style to his.

One of the greatest threats to any higher-up's day is the constant threat posed by lower-downs who do not use their access efficiently. They ask for meetings before matters are ripe for decision or action. They write memoranda that add little to anyone else's knowledge. Their careless requests for information consume valuable time. Don't be like them. Your access to your boss may be limited, but whatever routines govern it, keep in mind that your boss's time is a precious asset. If you show an understanding of this, you are not likely to waste it. Appreciate her busy schedule and try to fit your priorities within that schedule in whatever way best suits her. For example, when I worked in City Hall, there was a specific time set aside each afternoon when I would bring a number of items to the mayor for his consideration or decision. This minimized interruptions and fragmented conversations when one or both of us was distracted or unprepared.

Your boss is entitled to know what is going on, but she is also entitled to your best efforts in helping her deal with any bad news. Higher-ups don't like problems dumped on them. That is why bad news often does not move up in an organization. No one wants to be tagged as the messenger. Rightly or wrongly, the higher-up often links the messenger with the message. If you learn about a problem before she does, try to deal with it before being tempted to deny its existence. Consider delivering the message with some remedy in mind. Don't just lay the problem, like a dead bird, at her doorstep and then steal away. If you were in her shoes, wouldn't you want some help? Maybe your advice or remedy won't work, but at least she knows that you take her interests seriously and not just your own.

Similarly, criticizing how higher-ups perform is something that all lower-downs indulge in, but few know how to bring it to their boss's attention. If your boss is insecure as a higher-up, criticism is especially difficult to broach. Still, if you are critical of how she manages, it probably means that your work and your well-being are being adversely affected. Short of leaving the organization, which is always a prospector's option, it makes sense to try to do something about it. Consider offering your criticism and making suggestions in such a way that again shows that you take her interests seriously. You're not there just to whine about yourself. What she needs is the sense that you understand her priorities and have taken them into account. Then she is likely to listen; she is also likely to have good reason to consider and even act on your advice. The differences between you may very well center on who does what.

Who Does What

Prospectors who want to get ahead don't have a lot of time in an organization to make their mark. How they manage their relations with higher-ups has a great deal to do with the opportunities they get. One thing leads to another. Getting ahead means getting higher-ups to give you enough challenging assignments so that you can show your talents off to good advantage. You should understand, however, why they may find it hard to delegate such work. Put yourself in their shoes.

1. Even though higher-ups prefer to get timely help, many of them can't find the time to bring lower-downs up to speed so that whatever needs doing is not compromised by someone they consider less knowledgeable or less experienced. A higher-up has a broader network of information sources and may hesitate to share the intelligence gathered from such sources. He doesn't delegate much simply because he knows more or knows better how to get something done.

2. Higher-ups know that delegating a piece of work does not absolve them of responsibility for the outcomes produced. From their point of view, why take the risk of letting some-

one who they think is less capable handle an unpredictable situation? Whatever happens, they are accountable to their higher-ups for particular tasks, delegated or not. They remain at risk for what is done on their behalf.

3. Higher-ups think that they have good reason for hesitating to delegate certain matters if a VIP, inside or outside the organization, is likely to feel snubbed. When a higher-up delegates a task, it is often difficult to delegate the authority necessary to impress others. It does not matter that a lower-down has his complete confidence. He worries that the lower-down may not be able to command the confidence of those who have come to expect attention from the higher-up, not a subordinate.

4. Once we lend what we have to others, it is hard to get it back. Delegation is like that, and it is why higher-ups may hesitate to part with certain functions or share them. When my daughter was in college, I lent her my small four-door compact, which she did not think was getting enough use. She made good use of it, but then I discovered that the tires were shot (she forgot what the correct air pressure was supposed to be), the engine maintenance was suspect, and the interior looked like a traveling garage sale. I wanted the car back, but she insisted the compact now more or less belonged to her. I was faced with rooting for my car or for my daughter. As usual, she won out. A higher-up knows there is a risk that the delegated work will not be properly cared for, and if he reclaims it, it may cause a breach with the lower-down that is difficult to repair. No one, higher-up or lower-down, likes to look bad by having something taken away that they thought was theirs, even if it was only lent to them. A higher-up may even go so far as hiring additional

people to get delegated work done because he doesn't want to confront the lower-down who can't do it right. Three people end up doing the work of one, and who is going to complain? Only the higher-up, and he has already declined to do so.

Having put yourself in the shoes of a higher-up to appreciate why he may find it hard to delegate, it also makes sense to help him see it from a lower-down's point of view. Obviously, when work is not delegated, he gets overloaded, you are underutilized, he gets stressed out, and you may suffer the consequences. A working relationship may also founder when a higher-up simply gets rid of tasks that he doesn't want to do, or he invents make-work projects that have no perceived value, or he gives the same task to several people, causing suspicion and confusion about who is actually needed to get it done, or he brings in an outside consultant to do what insiders think they are competent to do themselves. If your boss employs one or more of these stratagems, it probably means that he has given little thought to developing the talents of lower-downs.

If a higher-up has not considered the importance of staff development, then delegation is not likely to work very well. Lower-downs find themselves constantly checking back, seeking approval before proceeding further, unwilling to take risks with someone who is only concerned with results. One way to get a higher-up to delegate more is to make the case that your development can help him. Put it in terms of his interests, not just your own. Ask for assignments testing your skills that build confidence. As your confidence improves, so will your performance and his confidence in you. If he is results-centered, your appeal should square with his self-interest.

Ask him to imagine what he would do in the event of his prolonged absence. Or, as one prospector to another, ask him what his departure would mean for the organization. If he thinks about such events and sees that many tasks will be left undone or not done well, then he has good reason to plan ahead by developing the talents and experience of those most likely to fill in or succeed to some of his responsibilities. Grooming a surrogate or successor can't be done effectively at the last minute. Your hypothetical question can help him anticipate what adjustments he needs to make, such as taking time to share information on a regular basis—dumping memory, as some people call it. Lower-downs have to be in the loop needed to get delegated work done. You can only be up and running with information that he has invested in you day in and day out.

He can also help himself if you suggest that he rehearse with you on how particular delegated work might be done. If he does, both of you are more likely to know its prospects for success, whether it is getting a project under way, developing a new office policy, or organizing a team to address an urgent problem. He may have unrealistic expectations of your performance unless he considers with some care how he would go about doing the work himself. A good rule for higher-ups in an organization is: "When you ask people to do something for you, be sure it can be done. Try it on yourself for size. If you merely say, 'here it is, get it done,' you may not really know what you are asking of them."

A higher-up should also clarify what is delegated and what is not. I would ask staff members to tell me in their own words what they understood was being delegated. I couldn't be sure whether my instructions had been clear or sufficient. It was equally important for me to clarify what was not delegated. I wanted to be consulted when money, or VIPs, or the press and media became involved. Ask your higher-up to do the same thing. It may not occur to him and that can create unnecessary problems between you.

And let him know that his regular feedback will avoid any checking-back anxiety or the risk of having to improvise on your own. Most delegated tasks are not fully developed at the outset— new things happen, relationships get complicated, time frames need adjustment, crises erupt. Try to get on his schedule on a regular basis so he can monitor the progress being made and bring his information, resources, and authority to bear on your behalf.

Take another look at the problems that you encountered at Brash Venture, Inc. in the Chapter 1 vignette. What can Brash, Speedo, and Spandex learn from you about who does what?

Preparing for Meetings

Too often people go to meetings with little appreciation of what they are getting into. This is really not a productive use of anyone's time. Meetings involve complicated interpersonal and group dynamics that can surprise the participants and derail their proceedings. Preparing for such a game is never-ending but necessary work, considering that some people in an organization may spend between one-half to two-thirds of their time in meetings with lower-downs, with higher-ups, with colleagues from other departments, with vendors, consultants, auditors, outside constituencies, and on and on. Your preparation includes knowing what you want out of such meetings and understanding what others want as well.

Start with asking yourself some obvious but often overlooked questions. What do I want to accomplish? What outcomes am I seeking? Whom do I want at the meeting? Where and when should the meeting be held and why? What should be on the agenda and in what order? Meetings, of course, can be organized around these questions, giving those who attend a chance to build the agenda with you, but most people don't have the time for such preliminaries and prefer that whoever convenes a meeting knows what they're doing in advance of the sit-down.

If a higher-up asks you to conduct a meeting, do you know what her intentions are in wanting a meeting and what outcomes she wants? Whom does she want at the meeting and whom does she not? What boundaries does she want for the meeting, that is, what topics are *not* on the table for discussion? Regardless of whose meeting it is, yours or hers, it helps to do some reconnaissance to find out what others' expectations are by touching base with the key players who will attend or send their representatives. You may discover that one or more of them have agendas of their own that they would like to advance.

Every meeting is an opportunity for anyone at the table to get attention paid, willingly or unwillingly, to a particular cause or complaint, whether or not it is on the agenda. And the less an organization attends to such causes or complaints in the normal course of business, the more likely they will pop up in meetings, like an ambush set for unsuspecting travelers. The ill health of an organization can often be diagnosed by just observing the conduct of those at a meeting who use the forum for their own purposes unrelated to the business at hand. Your premeetings with key players who will attend gives you a chance to hear their frustrations on matters that are not scheduled for discussion but may emerge anyway. You may also learn about conflicts that they have with some of the other players who will be attending.

Sometimes it is possible to avoid such problems if you audition them in the premeeting, so that a player feels that he has had a chance to vent his frustrations and will not feel compelled to do so in the meeting, where his outburst may sidetrack whatever you are trying to accomplish. And in your premeeting together, you may be able to suggest other ways to deal with his complaint or conflict with another player who will be at the meeting. At least he will know that his repeat performance at the meeting of what was auditioned in private will seem gratuitous and unwelcome to you.

If key players cannot attend the meeting, brief them as best you can as to what you hope to accomplish. What you want is to reach some tacit or explicit understanding that you share similar objectives for the meeting and that the representatives they send will work with you. Otherwise, representatives may be overly partisan looking after the interests of their higher-ups rather than the productivity of your meeting. Just letting a lower-down know that you have already talked with his boss can make a big difference in his behavior at a meeting.

If you are not able to garner premeeting support, you may want to reconsider your objectives or whether the meeting should be postponed. In any event, if you have to postpone the meeting, your preparation should include touching base again with the key players if enough time has passed or events have intervened to make you less sure of any understandings you reached with them earlier.

If there are written materials for a meeting, try to provide them to the participants in advance. A PowerPoint presentation should supplement, and not be a substitute for, any underlying documentation of an actionable item on the agenda. Nothing is more suspect or self-defeating than asking people at a meeting to discuss or approve of something in writing that they have not had a chance to read. You may get away with such an oversight, but you will probably pay for it at some later point, when one or more of those who attended show little understanding of what they were asked to approve: "I had no idea *that* was part of the proposal." You want people to have enough information so that they can think about agenda items before the meeting, not as a fuzzy afterthought when they leave. Sometimes it is tempting to get prompt action at a meeting by denying others the information they need to raise reasonable objections. But assuming they will get their say later, why try to slip one past them in the meeting? What do you really gain, and is it worth risking a breach in your working relationships?

If you are passing along written materials that were prepared by others, it helps to know who actually wrote the memos or reports that you are relying on and perhaps talk with their authors before the meeting, especially if they are not planning to attend. It also helps to note who was "copied" on any document that you plan to use at the meeting. Such detective work gives you a better understanding of why the document was written in the first place and how much it has already been circulated inside and outside the organization. If you don't do your homework, others at the meeting may have done theirs and raise questions or objections that throw the meeting off track. It never hurts to overprepare. If called for, your command of the subject matter gives those attending more confidence in you and what they are being asked to do.

The setting for a meeting and where you locate yourself in it are important symbolically. Should you use an informal working space familiar to everyone, your office, or someone else's office? Where do you sit—at the head of the table, behind your desk, or in a circle of drawn-up chairs? I don't have the answers, but you probably do if you remember to ask yourself these questions.

What is the best time of day for a meeting? I think it is whenever the key players, who you want at the meeting, can come. To schedule a meeting that suits your convenience or your higher-up misses the point. You need others' attendance and cooperation or you wouldn't be having the meeting in the first place.

How many people in a meeting are too many? If you want to be inclusive, then leaving people out defeats the purpose of the meeting. If, on the other hand, you want the meeting to be productive, then more than eight to ten may make it unwieldy, assuming that you want their active participation.

How long should a meeting last? Any meeting more than ninety minutes may be too ambitious, given the attention span of those less interested in being there than you are. Notice who comes to the meeting on time and who does not. Are such entrances an accident of scheduling, or do they tell you something about a player's interest or intentions? Who leaves a meeting early is also worth noting. The timing of exits may tell you how well or badly the meeting is going from perspectives other than your own.

A meeting's outcomes are shaped by how well you prepared yourself and others in the premeetings and by the dynamics of the meeting itself. Try to organize the agenda and conduct the meeting so that cooperation develops and is not threatened from the outset by a badly timed piece of business. Don't let the first agenda item be something that immediately divides the players or distracts them, such as everyone reaching for their appointment diaries to see when the next meeting can be scheduled. You can waste a lot of your time together dithering about when you can get together again.

Consider starting with a piece of business on which everyone is likely to agree or has a chance to offer an opinion. You want to build a sense of constructive accomplishment among the players, temporary as their identification with each other may be. The order of the agenda can help to promote such collaboration or undermine it. Have you ever seen a meeting go haywire after an ugly skirmish among the players that could have been avoided? No one came looking for trouble, but an ill-timed agenda item set things off. In any event, it rarely makes sense to leave the most important item on the agenda for last when the energy of a meeting has already dissipated or participants on whom you are counting have already left.

If a consensus is reached in a meeting, take the time to restate it as best you can so that those attending have a chance to agree or disagree with your interpretation. What good is it to assume you have agreement in a meeting, only to find out later that a number of players are not on board? Ask for dissent. Don't assume that silence is golden. If no one seems to be in disagreement, soliciting their opinions may make some participants more reluctant to air their reservations later outside the meeting.

If a matter discussed at the meeting is best kept confidential from those not in attendance, make that clear before the discussion gets underway, or, at least, before the meeting is over. There is no guarantee that the participants will keep it confidential, but it may avoid misunderstanding and the excuse: "Oh, I didn't know we weren't supposed to discuss that with others."

The follow-up after a meeting is as important as the preparation for it. Try again to have one-on-one conversations with key players, this time to get their feedback about the meeting and your mutual expectations for following through on whatever was discussed or decided. If another meeting is to be scheduled, they should be consulted so that you can determine who can attend and what the meeting dynamics might be, given those who are likely to be there. Your preparation for a meeting is ongoing with premeetings and postmeetings to keep track of others' preferences and to communicate your own.

> **SHARE/CARE:** Read the SHARE/CARE vignette and then consider what you would do to prepare for the meeting with Tamara Jones of the Bridge Foundation, a meeting that the executive director has asked you to organize.
>
> No one associated with SHARE/CARE looks forward to the meeting with Tamara Jones next week, but everyone will

be there. Jones, as president of the Bridge Foundation, which has been the primary funder of SHARE/CARE in the first three years of its existence, will soon decide whether funding support will continue or not. The Bridge Foundation normally provides the funds necessary to get a project in place but expects that a broad base of support will be secured by the end of the initial grant period.

SHARE/CARE, a nonprofit agency, collects excess food and distributes it to soup kitchens, drug rehabilitation centers, homeless shelters, and other programs for the hungry. Some staff members calculate that in just three years it has provided about 2,500 pounds a day of leftovers from some of the finest restaurants and hotels in Gotham as well as from grocery chains and corporate suites. Molly Schmidt, executive director of SHARE/CARE, has fostered good relations with food vendors and celebrities to bring attention to her harvest agency, but she has spent little time finding a reliable source of income to support overhead in the event the Bridge funding is not renewed. Food vendors have provided food and celebrities have provided publicity for the cause, but such contributions have been in-kind gifts.

Although Schmidt has made many friends for SHARE/CARE, she has also had little time for the pedestrian work that might improve the efficiency of the organization. Somewhat insecure in her position because of her young age, Schmidt has not encouraged her borough coordinators and field staff to bring problems to her. Preoccupied with socially hustling restauranteurs, corporate execs, and the charity crowd, the executive director has not paid much attention to the problems of vehicle maintenance, food that has spoiled because of refrigeration breakdowns, theft, and pilferage.

Recently, Brindell French, a noted Gotham restauranteur and chair of SHARE/CARE's board, decided to help Schmidt by paying, out of his own pocket, the salary of an executive director's assistant who has more time for day-to-day operations. So you were recruited to join SHARE/CARE at a salary rate higher than most of the borough coordinators. Chief among them is T. J. Murillo, an outspoken and idealistic veteran, who has been an advocate for the homeless for many years. Murillo has no peer in recruiting volunteers or in public speaking, although, by his own admission, he is more a "mover and shaker" than a line manager. He once went before SHARE/CARE's board objecting to the Bridge Foundation support, since some of its money came from the chemical industry that made Agent Orange for use in the Vietnam War.

Murillo's most recent initiative to feed the homeless is to have SHARE/CARE augment its program by financially underwriting the publicity and coordination of a food voucher program. Neighborhood residents would be asked to buy food vouchers at local stores that would entitle the bearer to an equivalent value in foodstuffs. Such residents would then give the vouchers, instead of cash, to those who are soliciting money on Gotham's streets. Molly Schmidt, however, has told the board that street people might barter their vouchers for liquor and drugs, and SHARE/CARE's reputation would suffer if it were held responsible for such an outcome. The board has taken no action, but Murillo does not consider the issue closed.

One of your concerns with Murillo and some of the other borough coordinators is that they have not kept up with the paperwork that would help buttress SHARE/CARE'S case in the Bridge Foundation's evaluation or other prospective funders. Like Schmidt, the borough coordinators have been more interested in finding food sources and distributing what is donated than in keeping adequate records. Another of your concerns is the turnover of dispatchers in each borough, who have the important job of coordinating daily pick-ups and drop-offs of their perishable cargo. It is a difficult job and the pay is very little. When there are vacancies, Americorps volunteers have filled in, but they also come and go rather frequently. When you talked to Schmidt about the problem, she shrugged and said that a nonprofit organization such as SHARE/CARE has to put up with the turnover, since there never is enough money to go around.

This week, however, Schmidt seems more willing to listen to you, knowing that your concerns may very well be those that Tamara Jones will bring to the meeting. Schmidt also realizes that the agency may have to lay off a number of staff if Jones is not happy with what she finds next week and there is no renewal of funding. If there are staff cutbacks, can SHARE/CARE maintain its well-developed sources of supply with the demand so pressing in Gotham? It never ends.

Getting the Commitment of Others

If you are a prospector, you are probably not interested in committing yourself for too long to any one organization. You may find, however, that higher-ups are counting on you to help them build commitment to their enterprise. There really is no conflict. After all, what others want for an organization can be very different from what you want for yourself. Understanding that lets you use your talents to further their interests, and if you succeed, it follows that they will be in a position to further your interests, too.

The traditional model of building commitment to an organization with a well-defined culture is to examine the fit between the preferences that people bring and what the organization already values. If the alignment is not good, the organization declines to hire such people or brings them on but reorients their preferences, so that they can adapt to the organization's priorities.

The reorientation begins in the selection process itself when a person is made to feel that she or he is joining a select group of people committed to a specific or exemplary mission. This is followed by socialization and training, as coworkers and mentors help new employees to understand and practice what is expected of them in performing up to the organization's standards. In addition, the rewards offered by the organization help to reinforce its particular norms, and the organization tries very hard to keep the promises it makes, like job security, in order to build trust, which helps to build commitment.[4]

Consider then how much harder it is to build loyalty to an organization when it makes no long-term commitment of its own to employees and when they have so many personal priorities of their own. Can working conditions satisfy such a wide range of expectations?

In addition, your colleagues can become fierce partisans for the section, department, or division in which they work. It may be much easier to get their grudging compliance with rules or routines than to get their willing commitment to the goals and objectives of the entire organization.

How then does an organization try to align these personal priorities and partisan interests with its own? There are a number of ways, although you have to be the judge of their fit for the organizational circumstances that you encounter.

Aligning Personal Priorities.   With job security more tenuous and job opportunities elsewhere trumping organizational loyalty, does the organization try to customize the work relationship to meet so many diverse preferences, whether for money, independence, gratifying work, likable coworkers, a pleasant environment, contributing to the public good, or career advancement?[5]

If money is a priority, does the organization have a variety of tailored benefits and bonuses? For those who value independence, is flextime or telecommuting available to accommodate their family lives and work schedules? If gratifying work is an important measure, are programs being developed to provide more education or in-house training to make employee skills more marketable? If the priority is for likable coworkers and a pleasant work environment, are there amenities, such as open floor plans, communal space, in-house food sites, plazas, parks, and day care centers, that encourage collaboration and friendships? For those who want to contribute to the public good, has the organization developed and sponsored outreach projects? This may be especially important when people are spending more time at the workplace and may have weaker ties to the communities in which they live.

Aligning Partisan Interests.   Can a strategic plan reconcile the various units in an organization? That depends on how the plan is developed. Are the planners only communicating with higher-ups? Are lower-downs being consulted? Are those needed to make any plan work being left out? If strategic planning fashions a destination and a path to get there without consulting the company troops who are to make the journey, it will look more like a forced march. A strategic plan has a chance of succeeding if there is employee commitment to the goals established, but that depends, to a great extent, on the kind of process used to shape them and the extent to which employees are included in that process.

Can a form of zero-base budgeting put an organization back together again? Such a process encourages the participation of lower-downs but asks that partisan departmental interests, which compete for limited resources, be put aside in order to rank the overall objectives of the organization. Does such a process offer an incentive for everyone to lay down their arms when everything is up for grabs? Does the process protect some of the hard-won ground that departments have secured for themselves in the annual line-item budget? Is there a focus on objectives without putting all budget allocations at risk again? Look again at the "Partnership Fund" vignette in Chapter 1. Did you think that the CFO's zero-base budget proposal would work at the Fund?

Can designing an incentive align partisan interests in an organization? It all depends. Imagine that you work in the central development office of Farflung University, and that once again the university did not meet its Annual Fund goal of raising X dollars. Each of Farflung's operating divisions, the schools of business, physical sciences, and social sciences, is too preoccupied with raising money for its own building and program needs. The Annual Fund drive solicits unrestricted gifts for university-wide needs, but, in Farflung's decentralized environment, partisan interests usually come first. Farflung's president suggests to you that if and when the Annual Fund goal is reached next year, then each division should be allowed to keep for itself all subsequent gifts to the Fund that it originally solicited from alumni and friends. Is it an incentive that will work?

When you design an incentive, its merit is not determined by what you or some higher-up would like to see happen. It depends on the expectations of those for whom the incentive is designed. The business dean may want the extra effort he expends on the Annual Fund to be returned to his division in some percentage amount, not after some threshold has been met. The social sciences dean may object because she does not have the kind of alumni prospects for Fund gifts that the business dean does, despite the proposed incentive to do so. The physical sciences dean may object to the effort level and risk in the expenditure of time required trying to raise money from sources who may prove to be elusive. When each division has different fund-raising capacities or expectations, it is difficult to treat them the same and expect that they will all respond favorably.

Designing an effective incentive requires putting yourself in the other players' shoes to see if it will work for them. Even better, let each of them try the incentive on for size. If the incentive doesn't suit their interests, then with their feedback perhaps together you can rework its design and get their commitment.

Voting and Bargaining

There are a number of problematic situations in an organization where no one is in control, and to resolve the players' conflicting preferences, voting or bargaining produces an outcome that everyone is willing to accept. On that much the players can agree.

Voting

When players call for a vote, they are signaling that they want to reach a timely outcome so that they can move on to other business. In a situation in which no one can dictate the outcome, reaching one that everyone can accept is no small achievement. But this does not mean that you have nothing more to think about except to raise your hand or cast your ballot. You want to consider whether the situation calls for sincere or strategic voting.

Imagine that you are part of a three-member hiring committee. Should the organization extend an offer to Black, White, or

Brown? Each member of the committee has a different order of preference:

	1st preference	2nd preference	3rd preference
Colleague #1	WHITE	BROWN	BLACK
Colleague #2	BLACK	WHITE	BROWN
You	BROWN	BLACK	WHITE

Since the three of you can't agree on one candidate, you do agree that the decision of the special committee should be settled by majority vote taken in a secret ballot. You also agree that in the case of a tie vote, the chairperson's preference will prevail. You draw straws, and Colleague #1 becomes the chairperson. If there was no further communication among the committee members, how would you vote?

If you cast a sincere vote for BROWN (your first preference), it is likely to produce a deadlock, and Colleague #1's preference for WHITE will prevail. Since WHITE is your least favored preference, you can, instead, cast a strategic vote for BLACK (your second preference), which creates the necessary majority with Colleague #2. It is the same thing that some Ralph Nader supporters tried to do in the presidential election of 2000. Not wanting George Bush to win, they decided to cast their ballots for Al Gore, their second choice. Such strategic voting, however, did not change the electoral outcome, unlike your strategic vote for BLACK, which will.

Making a distinction between two forms of voting, sincere and strategic, does not mean that such a choice presents itself in every voting situation that confronts you. Assuming that you make an effort to learn in advance as much as you can about the preferences of the other players, you have to take a fresh look at each voting situation—who votes, what are their preferences, what are your preferences, and what are the voting rules. You may determine that you can cast a sincere vote and that your outcome preference will also prevail in the voting, as Colleague #2 could do in the hiring committee's vote; or you may find that a strategic vote better serves your interests. It all depends.

For example, you may want to cast a strategic vote when there is the opportunity for "log rolling" in an organization. Log rolling is essentially a trading of votes, a form of self-interested exchange. I vote for your interests in return for your vote, sooner or later, for my interests. Log rolling becomes desirable when everyone wants funding for his or her pet project but is relatively indifferent to anyone else's pet project. To overcome this mutual indifference, you trade votes—your strategic votes for their projects in return for their strategic votes for yours.

Bargaining

The object of bargaining is mutual gain. Even though the preferences of the players conflict, don't be tempted to think of winners and losers as if it were a zero-sum game. It is not. Of course, the outcome of a round of bargaining may favor one player or another, but the process usually does not work unless there is mutual gain. You should anticipate the other player's preferences not just to better serve your own but to reach an outcome that serves his preferences, too.

Before using the process of two-party bargaining, consider what the preferences of the other player are. Merely assuming that you are at odds is not enough. You may discover that bargaining is beside the point. To dramatize that possibility, I ask students to pair up and role play a scripted negotiation between Dr. Smith, a research scientist developing a vaccine to prevent a childhood disease, and Dr. Harper, a research scientist who is working on a project to neutralize radioactive fallout. Both scientists need the veginot, an experimental melon that is in short supply. If the paired students inquire about each other's specific interest in the veginot melon, they discover that Dr. Smith needs only the seeds and Dr. Harper only the rind.[6] What often happens, however, is that both students assert the overriding social importance of their respective projects, taking for granted that their interests are incompatible. Such "sincere behavior" does not serve either of them well in the bargaining that becomes passionate and heated. If they use strategic thinking, their mutual gain is assured.

A bargaining situation usually favors the player with more or better information. Think of a seller who does not disclose the cost of producing an item for sale or an employer who does not open the company's books to employees seeking a salary increase. Both have a distinct advantage. Even when there is nothing to bargain over, it should still matter whether you have sufficient information to evaluate the outcome. If a higher-up were to divide a year-end bonus pool, it should make a difference to you what the total amount of the bonus pool is.

When players have the same information, they may be interested in more than just a price or salary offered. Does a price or salary offer appear reasonable, given what each knows about the other player's cost of production or profit margin? A potential buyer may think the item is overpriced, and an employee may think she is undervalued. It is not just a matter of the players agreeing that they are better off with something rather than nothing, but whether the bargain is considered fair.

In bargaining, what matters is not just what you want and think is fair, but what the other player wants and thinks is fair. Mutual gain may be out of reach if there is a serious difference of opinion. Some players will forgo gain rather than accept the short end of the stick. Try to ascertain at the outset whether you are both playing the same game. If one of you is centered on economic gain and the other is more concerned with principles of fairness, a stalemate is likely to arise. A bargaining stalemate often imposes costs on everyone involved. Consider, for example, the effects of a damaging strike when the ultimate settlement does not fully compensate for lost profits or lost wages. An ugly bargaining situation can take on a life of its own, and mutual gain gets shunted aside.

Finally, what happens *after* a bargaining situation is concluded can change your thinking about what gain you actually extracted from the process. Consider what happens when a buyer later discovers the seller's low cost of production or the employees later find about their employer's high profit margin. It may substantially influence any ongoing bargaining relationships. Mutual gain is not just tied to what each player gets in a bargaining situation, but how good the bargain looks in hindsight. When you reenter a bargaining situation with the same players, all of you may want to account for what happened in previous rounds before seeking a new outcome together.

I always remind myself when buying a stock whose prospects interest me that someone is equally interested in selling it. Similarly, getting the best of someone in a bargaining situation may not turn out to be such a good thing for you. To think of yourself as a winner treats someone else as a loser, which may not be to your advantage in the long run. You may need their good will and support for a host of other things you want to do.

> **LOCAL 29:** As the newly appointed labor negotiator for Pennacook University, how would you go about reaching a settlement with Local 29? You expected to have a getting-to-know-you lunch with Gina French, the business manager of Local 29. Instead, you got a call from the security guard in

the lobby. "There are seven women down here in the lobby who say they are having lunch with you today."

"Rudy, are you sure there are seven? I'm only expecting one."

"Nope, there are seven," Rudy answered.

You turned to your assistant. "I guess we're getting French's entire negotiating committee." New to Pennacook University, you were quickly learning that French was not your ordinary union leader. You anticipated a possible strike of the newly organized union of clerical and technical employees, better known as Local 29.

Pennacook started learning about labor unions ten years ago when Dominic Cabral came out from Boston to organize the maintenance workers on the Pennacook campus. Cabral had moved up and down the Northeast, organizing on behalf of the Hotel Employees International Union (HEU), affiliated with the AFL-CIO. No one had worked harder than Cabral to form what became known as Local 30 of HEU.

Cabral made an attempt to include the predominantly female group of clerical and technical employees at Pennacook, but, at the time, they showed little interest in joining a union of truck drivers, groundskeepers, and custodians. Later he persuaded Gina French, a labor colleague from New Bedford, to start a campaign of organizing the clerical and technical staff. If they were added to the equation, Cabral saw even better days for the union.

Gina French had her own ideas, however, about how to organize on the Pennacook campus. She soon broke with Cabral and sought recognition from the parent HEU for a separate Local 29. And she succeeded where Cabral had earlier failed. Appealing to feminine consciousness, French worked hard to organize around the idea of equal pay for jobs of comparable worth. As the male-dominated Local 30 obtained better and better salaries for its members, the unorganized women at Pennacook had suffered terribly in comparison. Now, as members of Local 29, they were about to negotiate their first contract with the university.

"Listen, I don't want to do all the talking," French said during the brown-bag lunch. "I want you to hear from the women who keep Pennacook going day in and day out."

Angela spoke first. "The average full-time salary for clerical employees is $25,000. That compares to truck drivers in Local 30, who average $32,000 per year, and custodians, who get $30,000.

Then Jennie followed. "I have a B.A. and an M.A. in English. My starting salary as an editorial assistant was $22,000. I hold a second job now to supplement my income. I have a ten- year-old daughter whom I hardly see anymore."

An older woman, Belle, put her sandwich to one side. "I have worked as a secretary for seventeen years at Pennacook. In that time, I have been promoted once. The man I work for started as a lecturer and is now a fully tenured professor. And he told me the other day that he didn't see the reason for Local 29. Imagine that."

"What did you tell him?" your assistant asked.

"I said, 'Professor so and so . . .'" Everyone laughed. "I said, 'Professor, you have your tenure and your department and your faculty senate, and I have my union.'"

The conversation passed to Ruth. "It costs me $600 per month for day care for my child. That leaves me $1,500 a month for rent, food, and taxes. I just can't make it unless we do better for each other."

"I can't afford to go on strike, but I will," Christine said. "I'll stay out as long as it takes to get a fair deal from Pennacook."

Finally, Alma, an unusually large woman, neatly smoothed and folded her brown paper bag and put it into the large purse she was carrying. Then she stood up and came over to your desk. Alma looked around at everyone in the room. "The union is women. Eighty percent of us are white and twenty percent of us are not. We are secretaries and telephone operators, we are research assistants and records technicians, but to some of the folks at Pennacook, we are," she hesitated for a moment, searching for the right word, and then said very slowly, "we are in-vis-i-ble. Now do I look in-vis-i-ble to you? No, I am not." She laughed good-naturedly and then, becoming very serious again, she continued. "I am not invisible, nor are my friends here. We are proud of what we do, and we have been overlooked for too long, too long, too long."

That afternoon you met with Sonya Manka, the VP for finance, and Nathan Sax, Pennacook's president. Manka had a bone to pick with her boss.

"Nathan, we're going to have a strike unless you stop talking about 'fairness and equity for all the members of the Pennacook community.' Local 29 thinks you're talking their language of comparable worth . . ."

"I'm not." Sax tried to defend himself.

"I know you're not, but it sounds to them like you are or, at least, that their crazy idea doesn't offend you. They'll grasp for any straw they can find."

"What's wrong with comparable worth? In theory, at least, it seems . . ."

"Nathan, you talk about fairness and equity, but in reality wages are a matter of supply and demand. Wage disputes are a normal part of a free market system. Comparable worth is not. A job, any job, has no intrinsic worth apart from market price. Local 29 is not talking about equal pay for equal work. They are talking about equal pay for work that is not comparable. How do you compare, how do you measure, Nathan, the worth of a truck driver to a secretary? You can't, but the market does. Not because the market prefers truck drivers to secretaries, but because the greater market value of the truck driver is established by the availability of truck drivers as compared to the availability of secretaries. And the wage differential becomes more pronounced when women come and go in the job market, unlike most men. It's not discrimination. It's a reflection of the choices women make about how they want to lead their lives."

You had listened intently to Gina French and her colleagues at lunch, and you did the same in the presence of Sax and Manka. Now, would they listen to you?

There are, of course, many ways to reach acceptable outcomes other than taking a vote or explicit bargaining. Chapter 2 explores tacit bargaining, Chapter 4 looks at the opportunities available when working with experts, Chapter 5 takes up the idea of finding enough others to change the status quo, and the Time Out, which follows this chapter, fills in what gets left out of most accounts of problem solving in organizations. Whether it is the problematic situations that I discuss here or those you actually encounter in your work, developing your talent to understand what others want is bound to make you a more productive and prominent player. I suspect you will find that many of your colleagues don't take the time or make the same effort as you do to understand the preferences of those they work with. Some of them may not know that it is even called for. So put yourself in their shoes. Do they need your help? From your point of view, do you want to help them? Think about it.

Storytelling in Organizations

Why We Tell Stories

I served on a jury during a steamy week in June a few years ago. At the conclusion of the criminal trial, we were left to weigh the evidence of whether the defendant was guilty or not of burglary charges. Our task in the jury room was to see if we could agree on what happened that day the defendant entered a downtown bookstore. Did he have a plausible reason for being in a private area of the store reserved for the employees when the assistant store manager confronted him rifling through a pocketbook? We all had been presented with the same evidence, yet we had different versions of what happened. More precisely, each juror told a story about what he or she thought happened.

The same kind of storytelling goes on in organizational life, although it is rare when everyone, like my jury, is working from the same set of facts. From most vantage points in an organization, it is often hard to know or explain what accounts for the outcomes we see all around us—the sudden departure of a key executive, or the launch and crash of a new venture. But just scratching your head or shrugging your shoulders to indicate "What was that all about?" is not much of a response, so we craft stories about what we think happened.

Storytelling is perfectly understandable behavior. We construct and reconstruct what happened in an organization to make sense of what otherwise might be incoherent. We organize the flow of our mutual experience into sequential episodes. "And then what happened" gives a narrator the liberty to tie events together that may not have been linked until the narrator's hindsight makes them so. The gift of storytelling is to identify, or even invent, cause and effect in order to make sense of the flow and to put the episodes in some order. It reminds me of the gyrations of the stock market, which the financial media try to make sense of by producing their instant storyline about what motivated investors on any given day. The pundits assign a cause for market moves, without offering the thousand other reasons why buyers and sellers traded shares that day on the floor of an exchange. A board of inquiry does much the same thing when charged to explain how some disaster happened in order to assign blame or to reform practices that contributed to the outcome. Whether the construction is the instant history of yesterday on Wall Street or the more methodical approach of the board of inquiry, it is, nonetheless, a form of storytelling.

Storytelling usually becomes a group effort in an organization, similar to framing a problem with colleagues (as discussed in Chapter 3), to understand why the key executive departed or what went wrong with the new venture. In constructing the organization story, each person may only have a piece to offer and little grasp of what really happened. There is a lot of guesswork trying to patch together what someone knows with what others know to create a coherent story. And sometimes one or more storytellers in an organization deliberately shade their accounts to avoid being held accountable or to place the onus on someone they don't like anyway. You and I do much the same thing with our own résumés, selecting those parts that we think others are interested in and leaving out a great deal that doesn't advance our personal narrative.

Storytelling bears some resemblance to the deliberate spin that official spokespersons use to interpret events with which they are all too familiar. Spin, however, is practiced by professionals skilled in partisanship on behalf of whoever pays them to be so. Storytelling is less organized and may have a dozen authors. Spin is a contest to mold opinion, while organizational storytelling is the accounts and speculations of everyday witnesses adding their two cents' worth.

Even though organizational stories are often less plausible than the storytelling that goes on in a jury room, it is important to listen to each person's version. They are telling what they care about, not just what they think happened. No one may have all the facts right, but what measure of the story is theirs is worth listening to. When we ask each other, "What is your take on what happened?" the question invites personal opinion and interpretation. The way a story is told and what is told belong uniquely to each storyteller. If you listen carefully, you can size up your colleagues, not only from what they tell you but also from what they leave out. There are probably as many opinions about the key executive who suddenly departed as there are versions for why he did so. If Jones liked the guy, then Jones may surmise that some higher-up villain forced the departure. If Smith didn't like the guy, then it's Smith's guess that the key executive never intended to stay around and finish the job. Jones' story leaves out his recent run-in with the higher-up villain over office space, and Smith neglects to mention that the departed executive turned him down for a salary raise last month.

As an organization's story is developed, it can serve the purpose of explaining the success or failure of colleagues or enterprises, so others can emulate or avoid such conduct. Such storytelling makes liberal use of cause and effect to underscore the lesson to be learned, although when there are many authors or many episodes involved, whatever lesson there is to learn is likely to be a mix of both substantial fact *and* substantial fiction. Nonetheless, higher-ups may find there is a moral to the story gleaned from actual events or events constructed to suit the moral, which they make part of the organization's folklore to be told again and again as a form of instruction. The launch and crash of the new venture may be finally attributed to the missteps of an outside partner chosen too hastily ("We'll never do it that way again"), or the official explanation may center on faulty software projections, assigning blame to the modelers, not the higher-ups.

When something significantly good happens in an organization, it is very likely that one or more stories will grow up around it. No one has time or gives much thought to what didn't happen. People give credence, albeit with some editing, to positive events. They invest importance and meaning in them. When, however, something significantly bad happens, the same people not only construct a story around it but are ready to tell of what might have been. When they invent a scenario that never took place but, in their opinion, should have, this is truly storytelling. Although they can never know the outcome of an alternative that was not chosen or a contingency that did not happen, that doesn't prevent them from preferring their story of what might have been. And there is some instruction even in such a fiction, if it gets others to consider what they might do to help construct a happier ending the next time around.

Like the board of inquiry that takes an outcome and reconstructs what it thinks happened, organization stories can also become part of an official version that gets passed on to outsiders for incorporation into news reports, case studies, or the management literature. Unfortunately, readers, investors, and other interested parties often get shortchanged. If you have ever read a news account about something you know more about than the reporter, you can understand how many amiable fictions get into print or are repeated in the media. When my work was in the public eye, I was struck with how often news stories, and that's what we call them, "stories," constructed plausible explanations about what I had done that didn't correspond to what actually happened. It has made me more skeptical about stories that I know far less about. While I don't totally discount what others report, I prefer later accounts from the actual players when they get a chance to set the record straight, assuming that they don't just offer up self-serving fictions. Autobiographies and personal histories of what someone did can be laced with generous amounts of make-believe. "Once upon a time there lived a virtuous leader in a treacherous land . . ."

Storytelling, then, is not just an idle sport for lunchroom conversation or something for the office grapevine. It matters what an organization thinks of itself, what its members do with their stories, and how outsiders interpret them. It seems to me worthwhile then to recount *what gets left out* of organizational storytelling—the accretion, drift, procrastination, search and innovation, mistake-making, and dumb luck. Choosing to tell you about the parts that organizations leave out of their official versions is not to debunk their success but to humanize their players. I think you should know that there is more serendipity than science to how things get done in an organization.

For the moment, put aside what the official stories tell you about how successful executives and successful organizations go about their business. A textbook account would have you think that their problem solving is a straightforward and transparent process—defining the problem, clarifying objectives, surveying alternative means, identifying probable consequences of each alternative, evaluating each in light of objectives, and finally making the best choice. It is easier, however, to draw a straight line in a textbook than to describe how problem solving works in most organizations. A textbook often diagrams the expectations of how "decision makers" should perform rather than what they actually do.

Too often we assume that higher-ups think before they act, that their actions are intentional, and, in short, that they know what they are doing. It is a comforting thought that pays a compliment to those who supposedly have problem-solving authority, but there are countless numbers of people who influence outcomes in an organization, and higher-ups rarely control how things gets done. They may not even know what options there are in advance of discovering them through action. What gets left out or obscured in most storytelling is how many things go awry or are unpredictable.

Can you trust me as a storyteller? I hope so. Everything I describe here has happened to me or is based on what I have observed across organizations and across sectors. At least, consider my unofficial version of what happens as a new starting point for understanding some of the outcomes in organizations that you go to. Over the years, students with full-time jobs have responded to my version with, "Aha, you're talking about the place where I work."

What Gets Left Out

Accretion

Some outcomes simply happen in an organization by small steps. The raw material for a story unfolds and progresses without anyone knowing that one is in the making. There is no author until someone constructs the story after the fact. Consider, for example, a customer service representative responding to an inquiry. The inquiry is answered and then shown to a coworker, who sees in it the gist of something worth changing in the customer service unit. A memo is written and passed along to another player, who uses it to make a larger point about product development, which leads a higher-up to initiate an internal review with far-reaching implications for the entire organization and far removed from the substance of the initial inquiry. A number of people, not necessarily knowing what outcome each wants or even aware that they are contributing to one, engage in discrete activities that address and ultimately resolve a range of problematic situations. It is not planned but evolves in circumstances in which no one thinks it through, much less walks it through the organization.

Of course, a storyteller may later ascribe an intentionality to all those who took part, flattering the organization and its performance. And what players would deny this rationalization of events if the story makes them look good? It is only when the story told is not flattering that they will look for the nearest exit, saying, "I had no idea," or "That was never my intention." They may even prefer to describe what happened as a hopeless muddle than to find themselves as prominent characters in a story that does not have a happy ending.

Drift

Drift in an organization leaves no discernible path to explain how outcomes are produced. Opportunities arise through timely accidents or unexplained adaptations that respond to a problem brewing or a solution hovering. The opportunity may come at a social occasion when two executives sit next to each other at a ceremony and decide to change how year-end bonuses are handled. It may be at a meeting of a committee that resolves a piece of business that was not even on its agenda. It may arrive with an outside consultant bringing a solution in search of a problem, neither of which an organization is even aware, or the opportunity may arise for an incumbent manager to repackage an old, rejected proposal and try to sell it to an unsuspecting newcomer-boss. It may be a press release that commits an organization to a course of action before anyone really knows how such a thing can be done.

Such drift is especially prevalent in undermanaged organizations, where players may be transients who come and go from the field of play. With little continuity or predictability in how things get done, problems that don't get attended to wander from one venue to another.[1]

I remember a choice opportunity that arose when I served on a temporary task force concerned with governance at the graduate school where I teach. I decided to press for specific measures to improve student retention, which I had proposed before at faculty meetings to an impatient or indifferent audience. To my surprise and pleasure, the task force welcomed the very same proposals because there was an immediate need to put some meat on the bare bones of an overdue report to the university's president. I discovered a choice opportunity neglected by others, and my proposals succeeded by default.

Don't think, however, that anyone on the task force would tell the same story that I have. They would tidy it up to maintain appearances that the task force proceeded deliberately and thoughtfully. The overdue report and my opportunism would just not be mentioned in a university setting, where people expect rational accounts of whatever happens. The only problem with such touching up, giving the story a facelift, is that an organization like mine is prevented from learning much from the experience. Of course, what I learned is to look for those occasions when I can frame a problem or offer a solution when few others care to do so or are even around to participate. I have to be willing to spend the time pursuing such opportunities in an organization in which my colleagues husband their time for altogether different purposes. Curiously, I find that my agenda of problems/solutions is better served by seeking out an occasion when there is less attention paid, rather than more, to their substance. Oh well.

Procrastination

Taking no action at all with respect to a problem is as likely to occur in an organization as the proactive scenarios that storytellers fashion. They think that they have no other choice, since, if there is no action, there is supposedly no story to tell. But when nothing happens, there still may be a story of executive procrastination. Such behavior is typical of higher-ups when confronted with undesirable alternatives such as which project must suffer budget cuts, or who should be laid off. Experience often recommends that they do nothing, at least for awhile. They simply put off action to see what else develops. They permit or invite interventions by others whose resources or ingenuity exceed their own.

Procrastination is not as bad as it sounds. I have often been rescued from what would have been a premature judgment and choice by waiting to see how key players reacted and what they proposed. To my surprise, their judgment and choices have often impressed me more than my own. So, instead of leading, I have followed. I was convinced, for example, that certain changes had to be made in the composition of the board of trustees with whom I worked as a college president. But I waited until the initiative came from them in shaping up their ranks, which made all the difference in how our delicate relationship developed. If I had pursued my shake-up, I might have lost allies and created new adversaries. Every higher-up has just so much personal capital to spend. It is easy to waste and difficult to replenish. I chose to save mine for another day. After the smoke cleared, I let the trustees tell the story, seeing no point in being part of it myself.

Newcomers and prospectors, who have no stake in the status quo, may become impatient with higher-ups who seem to ignore problems or postpone taking action. You may think that they lack time-management skills or are fearful of the consequences of having to make a choice, any choice. On some occasions, however, a higher-up may simply remain committed to a specific project or a favored subordinate and find it hard to let go or reevaluate. The "sunk costs" of time and resources already spent preclude a fresh look. The office talk may praise him for his stubborn determination while you see it as a blind spot that prevents him from changing course. As it turns out, the final chapter is likely to be told by new players, a freshly minted CEO or a reconstituted board of directors, who finally separate the higher-up from his pet projects or cronies. The former hero becomes the bad guy in the telling.

Search and Innovation

When I look for a gift in a department store, invariably a salesperson asks, "May I help you?" My usual response is: "No thanks, I don't know what I want until I see it." The store offers a richer and wider assortment of gift options than I can contemplate or predict in advance. The same is true of the complex environments of organization life. Contrary to the assumptions of some textbook models, higher-ups do not necessarily know what they want, and even if they do, they lack superior calculating minds that are the equal of their environments. Far from it—a higher-up is likely to settle for interacting with her environment rather than trying to subdue it. One commentator compares it to the scene of an ant walking on a beach. The ant's path may be quite complex, but the complexity of the path does not reflect the complexity of the ant but rather the complexity of the beach.[2]

When a higher-up sets out with the intention of getting something done, a search may best describe her path, which is not likely to be straight or of her own making. She is not fixed on a specific course of action or even a choice among several courses of action. Instead, she makes her way through the day absorbing soft data, engaging others in a problem, and taking advantage of unforeseen opportunities to educate herself and her colleagues.

If Cody Jackson tries to sketch her comings and goings in the vignette that follows, her crisscrossing paths look more like that ant on the beach than a deliberate journey. Her search has purpose, but, like my visit to the department store, she does not know what she wants until she finds it. Furthermore, a great deal gets left out of her story. Even if she tries, she has a hard time remembering all that happens along the way, much less being able to connect all the dots. Her editing is a way of making sense of the outcome, and like her erratic course, she eventually navigates the storytelling as best she can. What follows is the making of her story.

CODY JACKSON'S SEARCH: Ellis Doranian's corporate jet rolled to a stop near the hangar at Dolby Field outside Factory Hill. Larcom Semiconductor kept their company planes at Dolby, and it was a discreet place for Cody Jackson to meet Doranian. Through third parties, Jackson knew that Doranian and his Sun Belt Associates were still buying Larcom stock. Now he apparently wanted to meet Larcom's management.

Ellis Doranian, however, only spent ten minutes with Larcom's CEO in the small waiting room at Dolby Field. "You should know, Ms. Jackson, that we have a strong interest in Larcom. Before the rumors of takeover start stirring bad blood, I wanted to tell you that when I play, I play to win.

You should also know that I've already spoken to your major shareholder, Dominique Larcom. We've had some very fruitful discussions." Doranian then looked out the window at the little used field and the early morning landscape beyond.

Jackson had very little to say. She had suspected that Doranian's visit was only a courtesy call to impress her personally with the threat he posed. She escorted him back to the waiting jet. but she did not wave as it wheeled for take-off. "So this is how the story begins," she muttered as she eased into her limousine for the short ride back to headquarters in Factory Hill, an old textile city that now depended on tourism and Larcom, the only significant corporate employer in town.

As soon as Cody Jackson reached her office, she asked for Fritz Orlovsky, Larcom's vice chair and CFO. Jackson had known Orlovsky at business school, and, wanting some help at the top, she had recruited her old friend after Cyrus Larcom, the company's founder, died suddenly, leaving Cody in charge.

"Well," Orlovsky asked, "you met our newest shareholder. How did it go?"

"He wants the company," Jackson replied. He's already had 'fruitful discussions' with Dominique."

Orlovsky sat down hard. "Well, it'll be a hell of a blow to Factory Hill. If we become a subsidiary of some holding company, you can bet we'll lose the kind of decision-making turnaround that keeps our best people here. It's hard enough anyway to keep good engineers from job-hopping in this industry. Engineers and managers make up twenty percent of Larcom, and they're the ones who create the jobs for everyone else. I'm told that one engineer creates four jobs for the company and twelve support jobs in the community. If we lose that kind of productive spin-off, Factory Hill is back to hard times again."

"You're preaching to the faithful, Fritz. Let's have a small meeting with Ira Burroughs first thing tomorrow. You, me, Ira, Gretchen [senior VP and counsel] and Phil [VP for external affairs]."

The following morning Ira Burroughs was at the head of the conference table in Jackson's office. Burroughs, a young investment banker from Boston, had an air of authority about takeovers that the Larcom executives knew they lacked. Burrough's firm, First Mercantile Corporation, was a leading player in the recent takeover history of corporate America. Burroughs started talking even before the coffee arrived.

"First, let me tell you about Ellis Doranian. He goes after undervalued companies with mediocre management." Burroughs paused for a moment. "No offense, that's his opinion of Larcom, not mine. He claims to represent the neglected shareholders and tries to help them maximize their return. Doranian puts the a target company in play, and that means if Doranian does not win control, some other acquisition-minded company attracted to the scene often does succeed."

"Are there any antitrust angles to explore, Gretchen?" Jackson asked her counsel.

"Not really," Corso replied. "This is Sun Belt's first foray into high tech. Given their large position in oil exploration, maybe they want our microcompressor line and research to improve the efficiency of their production holdings." Corso paused. "Of course, litigation in whatever form often buys time, if that's what we need. At the very least, it drives up Doranian's costs if he's serious about a takeover. But in the end, the courts, by and large, prefer letting both sides go at each other."

"Look," Burroughs interjected, "your board has to consider, among other things, whether the company is worth more than whatever price is being offered. Let's say Doranian makes a tender offer at $35 a share. One way to measure the fairness of his price is to see if there are potentially higher bidders out there somewhere. If so, your directors reject the offer and do whatever is necessary to prevent Doranian from getting control of the company." Burroughs turned to Jackson. "We're running the numbers now, and we can make some inquiries about bidding interest after Doranian makes it official." Jackson just doodled on her yellow pad.

Phil Rexroth stood up and went to the board. "Cody, we should get Factory Hill involved. Work the downtown establishment, get everyone thinking 'save Larcom, save jobs, save our city.' Hell, we employ about ten percent of their workforce. That's five thousand households at least." Rexroth started talking rapidly as he marked up the chartboard. "We put together a Larcom Day Rally. Old Factory Hill against the Sun Belt."

"Maybe, Phil, maybe." Jackson waved her hand. "OK, we need to sort this all out." Jackson called Francis Moody, the president of the local Boot Valley National Bank, to confirm their dinner plans.

That evening Jackson and Moody met at the Old Fellows Club in downtown Factory Hill. Moody already knew about the Doranian campaign. "Cody, you know that Larcom is

Factory Hill's crown jewel these days." Moody hesitated for a moment.

"Speaking of crown jewels, Francis, I assume that the Factory Hill Partnership still wants first option on that large tract we own north of the City near Dolby Field." It had been made very clear to Jackson that the Partnership, a coalition of political and business leaders, wanted no airport or commercial development except on its terms.

"Nothing has changed, Cody," Moody replied. "Has it for you?"

"No, I was just thinking about it today."

Moody smiled. "Would Ellis Doranian buy Larcom just to cash in on your real estate?"

"I don't know, Francis."

Moody pushed aside his plate and said very firmly, "The Partnership likes Dolby Field just the way it is."

"OK, I hear you." Jackson finished her entree.

"You know, Cody, what you could use is a corporate ally with a very deep pocket. You and I have never talked much about the Atlantic Company. There is a lot of Moody family money still in there. We're not substantial, mind you, but the company goes way back with Factory Hill. As you know, Atlantic originated as a nineteenth-century textile company and left us fifty years ago for cheaper labor in the South. They're all over the world now. They diversified, changed the name to Atlantech Corp., and probably can't even spell 'textile' anymore. But Atlantech shouldn't be overlooked, Cody. If you'd like, I would be glad to set something up for you and their CEO."

"That might be a good idea, Francis. Let me call you in the morning after I've talked with Burroughs and our team."

The next morning the *Factory Hill Banner* sounded the alarm. Ellis Doranian was no longer copy just for the business pages, at least in Factory Hill. A *Banner* cartoon on the front page showed Doranian in pirate garb sitting atop the Larcom building. When Cody Jackson pulled her BMW into the reserved section of the company's parking lot, several employees were standing around in small groups, talking among themselves. One of them, a veteran of Larcom, approached the CEO.

"What's going to happen now?" he asked. Jackson put her arm on the man's shoulder and started walking toward the front entrance.

"Lou, we're not going to let some hotshot destroy what you and the others," Jackson pointed to those still standing around in the parking lot, "have done for the company."

Lou still looked bewildered. "Would Mrs. Larcom really sell her stock? I don't understand. This was Mr. Larcom's whole life. Can you talk to her?"

"I will. I'll be talking to a lot of people." Jackson opened the door for her employee as they entered the lobby of the Larcom building, which was wrapped in blue-green glass.

Ira Burroughs and his associates from First Mercantile were waiting for Jackson in the conference room.

Still standing, Jackson asked, "Ira, what do you know about Atlantech Corp?"

"One of the biggest and the best of the multinationals. We don't have any substantial relationship with them. What do you have in mind, Cody?"

Jackson thought for a moment. "If Doranian does want our real estate, perhaps we should sell it to someone."

"Atlantech?" Burroughs asked.

Jackson turned to Orlovsky. "Francis Moody told me last night that Atlantech may still have a fond spot for Factory Hill."

"First Mercantile could make the approach," Burroughs offered.

"No, I'll let Francis set this up," Jackson said firmly.

"Well, watch out for Simon Kirk, " Burroughs stood up now. "Atlantech's CEO is one shrewd dude."

Jackson started to talk quickly. "Gretchen, I want a directors' meeting for tomorrow by phone or here at headquarters, whatever can be arranged." Corso left the room. "Phil, call the *Banner* and tell them to keep the drumbeat going on the editorial page. Give them whatever they need." Rexroth scribbled notes. Jackson then turned to Burroughs. "Ira, I haven't ruled out anything, but I want to talk to Dominique Larcom and, I hope, Simon Kirk before proceeding. My directors are very sharp and very independent, and they won't jump through my hoop just because I'm the chair and CEO. Fritz thinks I'm crazy not to have more inside directors, but Cyrus Larcom always thought a good company should have a strong board."

"Just the same," Orlovsky said, fidgeting with his pencil, "old Cy never faced a hostile takeover, either."

"Well, it's too late now to change horses, Fritz. I'm off to see Dominique. Ira, I'd like you here for the directors' meeting, OK?" Burroughs agreed.

Dominique Larcom lived in the Overlook section of Factory Hill. She had raised two sons during the years when her husband was preoccupied with the company. At the insistence of his wife, Cyrus Larcom brought his two sons into the business, but as it grew, they quickly lost the favored position that their mother wanted for them. After

Neal was killed in a race car accident and Skipper drifted off into enterprises of his own, there were rumors that the Larcom marriage was finished. Then Cyrus Larcom dropped dead, leaving 15 percent of the company to his wife and surviving son. Dominique Larcom refused Cody Jackson's invitation to come on the board of directors. She didn't like Jackson or anyone who had joined the company in senior positions after her sons were denied promotion. She never visited the Larcom headquarters and was rarely seen in Factory Hill. She did a great deal of traveling and kept a home in Santa Fe. Cody Jackson had not seen her in two years.

"I still do not understand, Ms. Jackson, why we could not have this conversation over the telephone."

"Some things are better said face to face." Jackson followed her down the hall to a large dark library, where the oil portraits of her husband and two sons looked down on them.

"Mrs. Larcom, I gather that you are thinking seriously about selling your stock to Ellis Doranian."

Dominique Larcom looked amused. "You have always taken me for granted, Ms. Jackson. Why should you be concerned now with what I do?"

"I hope you will not tender your shares to Doranian."

"What makes you think that Ellis Doranian would be so bad for Larcom? He visited me in Santa Fe last month, and I found him to be competent, very understanding," Dominique Larcom paused for effect, "and very attentive."

"I'm sure he is," Cody replied. "But your husband built a company for people who wanted to capitalize on new ideas, bring new inventions to the market . . ."

"Don't tell me what my husband wanted or what kind of people he built the company for. I know better than you, Ms. Jackson, far better."

Jackson backed off and tried again. "What I meant to say, Mrs. Larcom, is that Ellis Doranian wants our company for short-term profits and perhaps to sell that tract of land we own near Dolby Field."

"I don't know what he wants. He didn't tell me. But he certainly couldn't be any worse than some of those smart-aleck M.B.A.'s who work for you now."

"You mean Fritz Orlovsky?"

"I mean all of those types down there." She pointed in the direction of the city. "There are no engineers in your senior circle, not a one."

"You forget, I'm an engineer," Cody reminded her.

"Oh, you gave that up long ago. Skipper and Neal and their father were engineers."

Dominique Larcom was lost in her own thoughts as she escorted her visitor to the door. Finally she said, "If that Dolby piece is sold, does that mean a major airport is coming to Factory Hill?"

"I can't say for sure, but it's one reason I suspect Ellis Doranian is interested in us."

Jackson hesitated at the door. "I know how you and your neighbors in Overlook feel about that prospect living so near to Dolby."

Dominique Larcom maintained her distance. "Oh, I don't know. I guess I can always sell this place and just stay put in Santa Fe. I rather like the Southwest, the Sun Belt, as you call it, Ms. Jackson." She opened the door for her. There was nothing more to say.

Inside her limousine, Jackson's driver had a message from Francis Moody. "He wants you to meet him at Dolby Field. Mr. Kirk is coming by helicopter from Boston."

Jackson stared out the window as they drove out to Dolby. She could not fathom what Dominique Larcom would do or why. Perhaps Dominique didn't know either. As the limousine approached the field, Jackson spotted a helicopter flying over what she knew to be the Larcom tract east of Dolby.

Francis Moody stood outside the waiting room. "Simon Kirk should be here any minute now."

"Does he always come on such short notice?" Cody asked.

"From the moment I called, he seemed interested," Moody said. "He apparently has been keeping closer track of Factory Hill and Larcom than I realized. How are Larcom shares trading this afternoon, Cody?"

"We're up from 24 this morning to 28 and a fraction. It looks like the market believes that Doranian is serious."

The helicopter hovered, then landed close to where the two were standing. Kirk got out, ducking under the slowly turning blades.

They entered the waiting room, where Francis Moody produced enough quarters so they could all get a soft drink from the vending machine. There was nothing much else in the room except two benches, which faced each other. Kirk wore dark glasses and sat stiffly on one bench, drinking his Sprite. "That's quite a piece of land you own, Ms. Jackson."

"It seems to get more valuable every day," Cody replied. I've detected more interest in the past twenty-four hours than in the past five years. Francis may have told you that it is one possible reason why Ellis Doranian wants Larcom."

"Why don't you just sell it to him?" Kirk replied. "Wouldn't that be easier for everyone concerned?"

"No, it's really not, Simon," Moody joined in. "The Partnership in Factory Hill has an understanding with Larcom." Moody started to explain the Partnership to Kirk.

Kirk interrupted him. "I know all about the Partnership. You know, Francis, you're putting Larcom in one helluva bind. These guys," pointing to Jackson, "may soon have their backs to the wall, and you're telling them that they can't bail out by selling one of their crown jewels."

"No, we're not saying that." Moody could be abrupt, too. "What we asked for and what we expect is a first option to buy that land instead of someone who doesn't give a damn about how this area develops. Overlook is practically within spitting distance . . ."

Kirk leaned forward with mock seriousness, "Overlook? Francis, I thought you changed the name of that neighborhood to Moody long ago." Moody wasn't amused. Kirk turned to Jackson. "This takeover business can be fun so long as you're not on the butt end, but that's where you seem to be right now, Ms. Jackson. Atlantech goes up and down this country and abroad buying and selling companies, divisions, assets, whatever fits with our strategic plans. I've never been in your position, but if I were you, I'd be looking for some help."

"I am," Jackson assured Kirk. "That's why we're all here, I assume. Would Atlantech consider taking a 10 percent interest in Larcom and putting two directors on our board?"

"I was thinking of something more substantial." Kirk stood up. "Francis knows better than I—Atlantech created this city. This is a special situation for us."

"What do you have in mind, Simon?" Moody tried to help out.

"Maybe 30 percent or selling the Dolby tract to us, or maybe both."

"What do you want with the Dolby tract?" Moody asked.

"Safekeeping, Francis. Larcom may have to sell that piece just to stay alive. Atlantech has no such problem."

"You'd still give the Partnership first option to . . ."

"Francis, what you must realize, as I'm sure Ms. Jackson does, is that a first option in this case would be at the seller's price, not the buyer's. So it would all depend on its value at the time and what you wanted to pay for it and so forth."

Jackson brought the subject back to Larcom. "If you want 30 percent of the company, can we get a standstill agreement that you won't launch your own takeover for X number of years?"

"That's, of course, negotiable." Kirk looked at his watch and then asked Moody for some change to get another Sprite. While he was at the vending machine, Cody Jackson bit her lip and looked at Moody.

Kirk came back and remained standing. "Ms. Jackson, you can call me if you're interested in pursuing this. I assure you that Atlantech is very interested in Larcom. Thank you, Francis, for alerting me to all this."

Jackson stood up. "I have a directors' meeting tomorrow, and I will certainly get back to you." Jackson and Moody started to walk Kirk back to his helicopter, but he waved them off. "No, no . . . the blades, if you forget to duck." Kirk ran a finger across his throat and climbed in next to the pilot.

> The helicopter rose slowly and then quickly slid east on its way back to Boston.
>
> Jackson turned to Moody. "Do you think he wants all of Larcom?"
>
> "Cody, that certainly was not my purpose in asking him to come out here. But I am sure that Atlantech is not going to sell out Factory Hill."
>
> Cody Jackson climbed into her limousine and lowered the window. "You're right, Francis. They only do that once every hundred years."

When it comes to innovation in an organization, a higher-up finds it impossible to plot the line from point A to a point B when point B is not yet known. There is just no prescribed path to follow for players innovating together. The interactions among them cannot be accounted for in advance. Imagine our higher-up at a pool table on which there are the usual fifteen object balls. She aims her cue ball at them and they scatter in all directions. After making the shot, she reassembles the fifteen object balls and tries to make exactly the same shot from the same spot. If the second shot varies from the first by only an infinitesimal amount, the paths of the fifteen object balls will vary considerably. Intent on stimulating innovation in her organization, she may set a number of object balls in motion but not know exactly where they will go. All she will know is that small variations in the initial conditions promoting innovation may lead to substantial and unpredictable deviations on what innovations emerge.[3]

If, for example, she is part of a software company, those along the path of innovation, like the object balls on the pool table, may include the customer support VP and customers, the marketing VP and distributors, the manufacturing VP and suppliers, the finance

VP and financial analysts who follow the company, and the engineering VP and key software engineers. The path of innovation is substantially affected by how the cue ball strikes them, and whether the web of their connections give rise to generative relationships—relationships that have the potential of bringing something new into existence.[4] Our higher-up does not try to impose a predetermined course or outcome. Instead, she gives permission and time for the game of innovation to be played, she encourages contact and exchange among the players, and she harvests from their dynamic environment. She is happy to profit from the unexpected. The innovation does not reside solely in the end product but in the chemistry among the players, the creative synergy of the process itself.

Whatever the innovation process produces, it is not an easy story to tell. It is not plotted in advance but rather gets played out through improvised actions and revisions—the stuff of unending e-mails, meetings, casual exchanges, and fortuitous events of every kind. If the story is told, it needs a great many authors to help make sense of it.

Mistake-Making

Even when a higher-up has some idea of what should be done, she may choose to remain tentative about her data. She may want to prolong the time it takes to settle on a course of action. She anticipates that she will learn from her mistakes. The textbook models dress up mistake-making by calling it "trial and error."

Think of a course of treatment that medical doctors pursue. They make a tentative diagnosis and prescribe temporary treatment interventions to see what works and what doesn't. They want more information, more feedback, and more time. Prescription quantities are limited, dosages are adjusted, side effects are observed. That is why a pilot effort of limited scope and duration may make sense to test an organization's receptivity. Like a doctor, the higher-up wants to do no harm and looks for organization side effects before proceeding further.

There is a lesson in the story of a successful Massachusetts youth services commissioner who took two years to educate himself and key players about changes in that state's reform schools for juveniles. When, however, he went to similar jobs in Illinois and Pennsylvania, he got into lots of trouble because he thought that he already knew, based on his Massachusetts experience, what needed to be done about the reform schools in those jurisdictions. What he forgot was that his learning experience in Massachusetts gave him the opportunity to prepare the public and its elected representatives for change. By acting too quickly in Illinois and Pennsylvania, he did not leave time to learn and garner support using trial and error again. He would have done better to do more "groping along."[5]

Textbooks prefer to highlight what works, not what doesn't. By telling only part of the story, however, they build up our expectations that we can somehow get it right the first time. It is easy to get this impression when stories about important discoveries and accomplishments leave out so much. You would think that great minds and great leaders stride from one mountain top to another when, in fact, their journeys are more problematic. They eventually get where they're going by learning from their mistakes. There are likely to be as many valleys as mountain tops. Besides, good storytelling is far more engaging when the protagonist occasionally stumbles—to err is human, and, as I noted, my aim is not to debunk success but to humanize the players. When they are more accessible, your potential for doing what they have done should seem more promising.

Dumb Luck

The opposite of mistake-making is dumb luck, which is another variable that gets left out of sanitized storytelling. Dumb luck is anecdotal and entirely unreliable, and since it cannot be replicated, the textbook models have no use for it. Unfortunately, when such anecdotes are not considered fit for consumption, the stories of how things happen get misshapen. They make us too confident of our powers and prospects. As a consequence, organization B tries to replicate a successful project of organization A, not knowing that the project succeeded, in part, because of dumb luck. Then, when organization B's project fails, its members scratch their heads and ask: "What did we do wrong?" Probably less than they think. The storytellers just didn't give them the whole story.

I remember when those of us in City Hall were able to negotiate a sticky labor contract and remove certain disappointing agency heads with little political resistance because there was a city-wide newspaper strike, so that newspapers were unable to generate the public backlash that can so often prolong and complicate such undertakings. No one planned on such a strike. It was just plain luck that none of us foresaw, although I don't remember anyone acknowledging it in telling and retelling the administration's story.

It's a shame that dumb luck has no place in organizational storytelling. Who are we kidding? Almost everything we do needs a little of it to succeed. That even includes prospectors with organization smarts.

CHAPTER 4

Working With Experts

Who are the people we consider "experts?" Think of the specialists you work with. Think of yourself. For some, specialization is a way of life, and for others it's just a way to make a living. The guy who develops a yield management model to fill seats on a scheduled flight is very different from the guy who sells the discounted ticket at the gate. Both of them have special know-how, but we usually reserve the designation of expert to those, like the modeling guy, who use esoteric knowledge, which is less accessible than the information that the guy at the gate works with. All of us, including the guy at the gate, like to think of ourselves as professionals in how we perform our jobs, but experts are those professionals who have become highly proficient by practicing a specialty that is remote from most people's training or experience.

At first blush, the chapter title, "Working With Experts," might seem to be an oxymoron. "How do I work with specialists who know something that I don't know and can do something that I can't?

Shouldn't I stand aside and let them do their thing? Isn't that the whole point of why we employ them or insource their skills?" Yes and no. Yes, a rough division of mental labor exists in every enterprise, but no, if that means just taking experts on faith from one assignment to the next. Prospectors design and modify their work relations on the run and largely on their own as they manage a project, work on a task force, or team up to pursue new ventures. Each undertaking is likely to depend on players with a bewildering array of special skill sets, and your performance and success may depend on whether you understand the essentials of what they do, whether you can determine their competence, and whether you can engage all their talents, not just their expertise. If you take nothing else away from this chapter, I hope it is the desire to break down the barriers that keep you from developing more productive relationships with them.

And if you think of yourself as an expert, don't be too quick to pass this chapter by. Just like everyone else, you are a nonexpert in most matters, so we all need a little help. We have become so mesmerized by our professional credentials or those of someone else that we neglect to explore new ways of learning about and relating to each other. It may even help you break out of a specialist straitjacket, which you see as limiting who you are and what you are capable of doing.

In this chapter, think of me as a recovering professional asking you to reexamine some of the assumptions that govern your working relationships, so that you can bridge the unnecessary differences between nonexpert and expert, regardless of which side of that divide you think you are on.

The Status of Experts

First, the obvious. All of us would like to have some kind of expertise, especially in a society in which an individual's economic and social status is usually hard-won and precarious. People really need you when you know something special that they don't, or you can do something special that they can't. Possessing a special kind of knowledge and skill is valuable property that can be sold in the open market. And that's what most experts do. If there is a great demand for their expertise and a limited supply, they may be rewarded quite handsomely. Scarcity and status become one and the same.

Next, some background. To get ahead and stay ahead, would-be specialists have, for more than a century, successfully organized a plethora of professional guilds to separate and elevate themselves from organizations and a lay public needing their services. The driving force behind their professional enterprise has been the American university, which has spawned new disciplines and reshaped old professions, casting its net wide enough to flatter and capture every kind of occupation and then dividing all of them into increasingly narrow specialties to enhance productivity and performance. There is a special status of having credentials in a professional guild whose formal knowledge and theoretical content is constantly being developed, contested, and revised in an academic discipline and university department accredited to graduate trained specialists. Many specialists, in turn, are examined and licensed by the state and then regulate themselves using a code of ethics and a national association of professional peers.

Think of each expert having a nonexclusive franchise, granted by her education and training, to market her skills. Although it is an employer or clients who offer opportunities to develop her expertise, she retains what amounts to a lifetime membership in her professional guild. She maintains loyal ties to such an association, perhaps more than to her employer or clients, as she keeps in close touch with developments in her field. There may be a number of professional events each year that she attends—participating on special panels, delivering technical papers, and networking with experts like herself. Such guild membership, like a union card, gives the expert entree into the job market and signifies that she has guild colleagues who will vouch for her expertise as long as she remains in good standing with them. In fact, her status throughout her working life depends, in part, on what they think of her ongoing performance. It is this professional peer-centered focus, rather than being employer-or client-centered, that is an important measure of her status as an expert.[1] Most people who are employed or self-employed don't keep such elite company.

An expert's skills, like anyone else's, require practice through repeated application of her formal knowledge for the benefit of employers or clients. With such practice she acquires tacit knowledge, the know-how that develops her expertise, making it more reliable and adding greatly to her standing in the eyes of others. Her tacit knowledge, like the unwritten rules of an organization, is not beyond your powers to understand, but it is remote, since it is based largely on her experience, which you have not shared. Tacit knowledge explains why a chess grand master can play fifty opponents at a time, moving quickly from board to board as he recognizes patterns of how pieces were positioned in prior games that he has played. He doesn't calculate from scratch what to do on each board but relies instead on what he has learned from his chess-playing experience, the advantage of his tacit knowledge. It works the same way for specialists whose experience, even more than their formal knowledge, accounts for their advantage. I don't know about you, but I prefer a surgeon who has practiced his skills on lots of people before he gets to me.

Having autonomy and discretion in what an expert does also enhances her status in an organization. An outside consultant takes for granted such privilege, but an expert on the inside expects comparable latitude. The status of expert entitles her to work with a minimum of supervision, responding more to colleagues who share her formal knowledge and expertise than to those in the administrative hierarchy. She may also have autonomy and discretion in hiring her associates, determining salary levels, and evaluating performance. Such professional peer groups often prepare their own proposals and secure their own contracts with very little oversight. Unlike the pooh-bahs in the organization's hierarchy, they don't need a big title or office. Their status entitles many of them to shape working conditions, choose colleagues, and scope out the work that most satisfies them. They do not so much seek power over others as to distance themselves from those who don't share their specialized competence.

Professional subcultures arise wherever these specialists set up shop and share space. Each subculture in its own space, and centered on similar training and know-how, can reinforce a sense of specialness and separation from other parts of the organization that don't share or can't appreciate what "those guys down the hall" actually do. In Chapter 1, I noted that subcultures exist independently of whatever official values prevail and may, in fact, thrive by being in opposition to how most people in an organization think and behave. This can certainly be true of a professional subculture whose members reinforce their distance from the mainstream by a casual dress code and a preference for working hours, often at night and on weekends, when there is less office traffic. To dress differently and to put in irregular work hours are small but telling signs of being able to take one's status for granted, at least so it may seem to those who cannot do such things without the approval of higher-ups. The status of experts allows them to be different. They don't have to worry about their fit with an organization and its higher-ups in order to stand out.

Understanding the Essentials of What They Do

What an expert knows that you don't establishes a distance between you and a certain kind of mystification that is certainly not to your advantage. It is much like a bargaining situation, discussed in Chapter 3, which favors the player with more or better information. Think of the way you feel as a patient under the care of a medical specialist or as a client following the instructions of the accountant who prepares your tax returns. They take their expertise for granted. They don't think of taking the time to explain the formal and tacit knowledge that informs their advice. And you probably never think to inquire about the sources that they rely on. It is much the same when working with them in an organization. How often have you let some specialist use elaborate numbers or esoteric language without asking for a translation? Instead, you nod your head knowingly or let the whole thing pass, not wanting to appear dumb in the eyes of other nonexperts who are nodding their heads knowingly. They may have no better idea than you of what the expert is talking about, but you can't be sure. So you remain silent to save face rather than ask for a translation that might help everyone learn something they didn't know before—certainly you, at least.

Now you can't possibly learn what experts know without going through the same rigorous training and practice that they have, and you don't have the time or reason to do that. But it is not beyond you to understand the essentials of what an expert does and how he does it. Why is such understanding important? Simply because an expert prefers "professional reasons" to work with you.

Let me explain. There are always subtle differences between what you want to accomplish and what a colleague thinks is worth doing. Your preferences are not likely to be the same.

Understanding, then, what others want (see Chapter 3) becomes a useful preliminary in any undertaking. And nowhere is that more true than with a colleague who has expert status. If you understand the essentials of what he does and how he does it, you can help to shape challenges that he considers important in his field and hold him to his standards for such work. Offering him professional reasons to acquire more knowledge, to improve his skills, or to gain more status in his field, does far more to motivate him than do appeals for increasing market share or improving the bottom line. Experts are not immune from such blandishments, but you truly engage their specialized talents by understanding what they want, not what you or higher-ups want. And as organizations rely more on expertise across organizational boundaries, offering professional reasons, instead of in-house objectives, is not only smart but becomes essential.

But I'm getting ahead of myself. Before you can offer an expert professional reasons to engage his interest, you have to ask him what I call "stupid questions." I deliberately use that phrase, because one reason we don't learn the essentials of what experts do is to avoid the embarrassment of revealing our ignorance. If we don't ask, maybe they'll think we know more than we actually do. Like the boss who bluffs that he knows what he is doing, it is easy for you to get in the habit of not letting on that you don't have a clue. Since an expert probably suspects that anyway, try broaching the subject very simply: "I realize this may sound like a stupid question, but what does a specialist like you actually do, and how do you do it?" You are not asking for a quickie tour through the arcane land of expertise from where he comes. All you are asking is that he tell you what his expertise consists of, making his knowledge intelligible using nickel-and-dime language. Any first-rate expert should be able to do that, and beware of those who won't or, even worse, who can't.

When experts have to explain themselves to others in simple terms, it forces them to put aside the private shorthand and vocabulary used by insiders and to find bridging language that connects with those who are on the outside looking in. They may even welcome such an exercise, like the physics teacher who introduced quantum theory to his students. "I went through it once and looked up only to find the class full of blank faces—they had obviously not understood. I went through it a second time and they still did not understand it. And so I went through it a third time, and that time I understood it."[2]

What experts know is often made esoteric by the technical terms, even jargon, created to help frame and define their field. It does not mean, however, that what they do is beyond the understanding of nonexperts. For example, if you were to ask me what the essential expertise of all lawyers is, I would tell you that lawyers are experts at using language carefully and precisely—drafting wills, contracts, legislation, and judicial decisions—so as to clarify intentions and resolve disputes. We are language makers and interpreters. We also act as advocates and deal makers, but crafting language is the coin of our realm, our essential expertise.

Now why would this clarification on my part be important to you? If you understand the essentials of what I do, you can describe work that needs to be done in terms that challenge me, to craft language suitable for your purposes. You offer me a professional reason for practicing my talents. In addition, when you understand the essentials of what I do, it helps limit your dependence on me. You can specify that you want me to craft language that expresses your intentions and meets your needs rather than expecting or letting me shape those intentions and needs for you. Too often there is overreaching by experts or mindless delegation of authority to them when nonexperts don't take the time to learn what someone's expertise really consists of and what it doesn't.

WHAT DO I KNOW?: It has been my experience that I know far less than other people think I do. Whether as a lawyer, a policymaker, or a professor, people assume that I have assembled storehouses of readily accessible knowledge that I can summon to answer their questions as if I were responding to a closed-book exam. Whether I ever knew what they want to know is unlikely. Professional education and practice do not lead me to stockpile formal knowledge for eventual use. No one's memory file has that kind of capacity, nor should it. Instead, such training and experience tell me where to find particular information or knowledge and how to use it. It is in the application of such information or knowledge, not in its warehousing, that I demonstrate whatever expertise I have.

All of this leads me to believe that other people probably retain far less formal knowledge than I think they do, and so we conduct our professional lives with a kind of unintended pretension. I mention it here, not because it is a condition to be exposed, but for its delicious irony, especially in academic life. If called upon, we share what knowledge we have and honestly quarrel when what we know is in conflict, but we don't think of asking for an inventory of what a colleague supposedly knows. This "live and let live" ethos is, in fact, an essential condition for maintaining the stability and diversity of the university as an organization. Anyway, if pressed, each of us can always go look it up.

"This may be a stupid question" is an act of verbal self-defense, but it does acknowledge your desire to learn something. It can serve as an ice breaker between you and an expert, and it can lessen the distance between the two of you, whether he is a software code developer, a designer of financial derivatives, or a highway traffic engineer. This detective work not only helps you understand what he does, but, in the best sense, it also flatters him and may make him more responsive in working on problems and projects with you.

Your colleague and expert may, in fact, have some stupid questions of his own. He may find it difficult to improve his skills in a work environment that he doesn't understand. You may very well be the source of information that he needs to appreciate better the nuances of the project that you share, the preferences of decision makers to whom you are accountable, and any norms of the organization that may prove resistant to his work.

Furthermore, experts who have the intellectual and experiential resources that you need may lack the organizational resources that they need to maximize their performance. If you understand the essentials of what they do, you may be in a better position to help broker such resources. For the software developer it could be *time* to work with genetic programmers and new evolutionary software, for the designer of financial derivatives it may be the *data* needed to customize an options price model for hypothetical customers, and for the highway traffic engineer it could be the *access* to elected officials who hold the purse strings for a car-pooling experiment.[3]

Determining Their Competence

Asking questions, whether prefaced by "stupid" or not, acknowledges a mutual dependence between you and an expert, which makes it possible to build some initial trust. Mutual trust, however, usually comes from working with someone and evaluating his performance over time, like the routines you share with other colleagues day in and day out. You are not likely to do that with an expert. Learning through trial and error who is first-rate at what he does and who is not may prove costly when you are relying heavily on someone's expertise. It may be a game with only one round, not the multiround game in which trust has a chance to develop. In your personal life, an architect designs a house for you only once, and you expect a surgeon to operate, sew you up, and that's it. When you engage an expert, you would like to be more or less certain in advance that he can help you and that he is competent to do so.

How then do you determine an expert's competence before you entrust a problem to him? Asking stupid questions is a useful place to start, but it's one thing to learn the essentials of what he does, and another thing altogether to know whether he is good at what he does. There is no magic bullet that I can offer that totally answers the competence question, but let me suggest several ways of trying to satisfy yourself.

An expert's reputation is one place to start. Since the status of experts is determined, in large part, by their standing among their professional peers, you want to go to those who share the same expertise but who have nothing at stake in your undertaking. Keep in mind that the self-regulation of professional elites is not only to avoid government intrusion or oversight, but also to keep track of their peers so as to maintain the good name and status of their guild. They may be in a position to know just how good or not a particular expert is at his trade. They often have standards and measures that go beyond what the usual references offer—"I know him, I like him, I recommend him." Even in less organized pools of expert talent, there are usually outsiders, in academia, in government, or among foundation grantors, who are knowledgeable about who the standouts are and who are not. It takes some detective work, but it can be done if a lot is riding on having the right person for the job.

The reputation of an expert, like anyone else's, also depends on the opinion of those he works with. You can make inquiries with those in the organization or elsewhere who have worked with him. Were they satisfied? Were their needs satisfied? This assumes that they knew what those needs were and did not let the expert so dominate their relationship that he framed their needs for them. In the hustle and bustle of experts selling their advice and services, it is easy to forget that trust begins by feeling confident that an expert is looking after your interests and not just his own.

For example, you should be ready to ask the impertinent but important question of whether his expertise is actually needed for the particular problem confronting you. You can't take for granted that he will volunteer that information. As the saying goes, when all you have is a hammer, everything looks like a nail, and you can't begrudge him wanting to practice his expertise. When an expert shows little or no restraint in wanting to get involved, it may mean that he lacks the judgment, or perhaps the experience, that you want. If surgeon #1 wants to practice his skills on my insides when there may be less invasive alternatives for what ails me, and surgeon #2 tells me that such a surgical procedure is not necessary, what does it say about the competence of the first surgeon?

Another measure of competence is how much an expert tries to use the capacities of his clients or his colleagues in an organization rather than just seeing their deficiencies. Right now I'm trying to find a financial adviser to help me determine whether I can make better use of my assets. How do I measure his competence to do so? He can show me his track record with other clients. That helps. I can ask others knowledgeable about such advisers in his firm or elsewhere how he ranks among them. That helps too. But making better use of my assets is not assured by just finding out what he has done for others. How much care does he take in learning why I want to make better use of my assets: a daughter in law school, the cost of housing in Manhattan, the plans my wife and I entertain for an eventual retirement? Does he take the time to explore how much I already know about various investment instruments, and how comfortable I am with risk? For me, his competence is not just bound up in what he knows and how he invests other people's money. A measure of his competence is how much he can learn about me to fashion a plan, a strategy, that I can believe in and partner with him to make it work.

First-rate experts do not try to create dependence but instead try to restore health, resolve disputes, find answers, and so forth, by engaging the effort and cooperation of their nonexpert partners. I'm sure the financial adviser whom I ultimately choose will know how to do that. An expert's competence is, in part, how he uses you, not just his expertise, to achieve what you want.

CONSULTANTS: When my students face a particularly difficult situation arising from a case they have read for class, the predictable response of some will be: "This calls for a consultant." They don't know how to resolve the problem, so they delegate it to someone who supposedly can. My stock response is: "That's too easy. Why are you so sure that a consultant can help you?" My suspicion is that the consultant answer is an artful way of students trying to avoid thinking through a problem on their own. They don't want to take the time or they want to play it safe. They are sure that there is someone more qualified out there who is ready to ride to their rescue.

No doubt an organization has to insource various specialized skills from time to time. Consultants also bring an objectivity, a detachment, by virtue of their being outsiders, which insiders cannot provide no matter how capable they are, if they are already entangled in a problem or have taken sides on how to resolve it. Looking to outsiders when there are capable insiders is not, however, a morale booster.

Sometimes a higher-up uses the status of an outside expert to give more credibility to a position that the higher-up has already staked out on the inside. The higher-up is not asking her to solve his problem but to take his side in how it should be addressed. He has framed a problem, identified his needs, and then looked for a consultant's support.

What is far less desirable is to seek a consultant, as some of my students do, to frame an organization's problem and identify its needs for you. This runs the risk of a consultant selling you advice that was originally developed for another client. The economics of developing any product or service involves start-up costs that are not easy to recapture unless the product or service finds a receptive market. It is no different for a consultant who may labor long and hard to solve one client's problem, only to find that there is no profit in it unless he uses the same solution for other clients.

A consultant can rightly argue that replicating what he does for one client may very well serve the next one because the solution has been field-tested. After all, like the chess grand master, he may see that an organization's problem resembles a game that he has played before. Nonetheless, it helps to understand why a consultant may be tempted to take a solution off the shelf, so to speak, rather than customize one that fits your needs better. It becomes a problem for you if his solution is not a good fit for your particular circumstances. He has to make a living too, but his solution should serve your interests as much as it serves his own.

If you turn to academics for whom consulting is a sideline, there is an altogether different problem. Even though they will take your money, they really may be performing less for your benefit than for those professional peers who are interested in the originality of their work, not necessarily its reliability. If you understand the academic's priority of seeking and maintaining status in his field, you may want to exercise some caution before swallowing his advice. He may be coming to your organization to experiment with a wholly novel and untested idea. Like a new drug, you might take the minimum dosage and carefully monitor the side effects. A pilot project or a trial period makes sense to test the efficacy of what he offers.

Be especially alert with any consultant who tries to tell you what the future holds. The risk that comes with such a consultant is that you may find yourself retaining his services to help you prepare for the future that he has predicted. The better way to think about the future is to consider the probabilities of where existing conditions are headed. Ask for a consultant's projections from which you can make your own forecasts or develop your own scenarios. Leave predictions to the professional psychics.

Engaging *All* Their Talents

Most professional specialists prefer to avoid routine organization activities that distract them from their work. I found this to be true in law firms, think tanks, and government agencies, and the aversion is most pronounced in university life. Academics dislike committee work, have little use for meetings, coming late and leaving early if they come at all, and are not enamored of most administrators, deans, or presidents, finding them to be tiresome and highly suspect. Overall, they do not see themselves as organization players. A particular departmental subculture looks after their individual interests, leaving the organization to fend for itself. The status of administrators, however, is no match for those who have job tenure for life, and students, given their transient status, have very little permanent influence. To an outsider, this description of a university may seem a bit daffy and of little consequence, but I mention it here because it is the culture in which most experts are trained and from which many take their cue on how to behave in the organizations they join or work with. Furthermore, many organizations are increasingly modeled on the decentralized environment of university life.

The organization costs of not making full use of such talented individuals are enormous. An obvious but neglected fact is that those who are talented enough to be experts are also talented enough to help an organization in other ways. Does the pursuit of expertise claim all the other talents they had before they became experts? Are they experts simply because they had very few other talents in the first place? I don't think so. There are many problematic situations in an organization that do not fit neatly into one discrete category or another, and all around are these perfectly able players sitting on the sidelines. Isn't it worth finding out what else they care about and what else they can do to engage all their talents, not just their expertise?

> **A RECOVERING PROFESSIONAL:** I was forty-three when I came to terms with several of my ambitions and took leave of public office and the practice of law. I thought of calling my mother and asking only half in jest, "Can I go now?"

After all, what mother doesn't want her son or daughter to be a professional? Still, I remember mine was wise enough to warn me, "Be careful what you want in life, David. You might get it!"

My impression then was that a smug consensus had developed among practically everyone I knew that being called "a real professional" was perhaps the highest possible compliment. If I claimed to be competent at some special task and put it to the service of others, such conduct merited unanimous approval. It did not seem to matter what I was competent at, or whose interest I served, so long as I was competent in what I professed to know and do. Professionalism, like the air I breathed, had become indispensable but rarely examined.

What gets left out when professional specialization becomes a way of life? Your individual gifts, opinions, and sentiments not subject to professional measure are largely ignored. I remember sitting at large conference tables watching specialists putting the finishing touches on a big corporate deal or a multimillion-dollar public project, each of them performing a very specific task but never being asked and never expecting to participate beyond the narrow boundaries of their acknowledged competence. I saw a financial analyst number crunching a set of anticipated interest rates, a tax lawyer whispering to her client about a forthcoming IRS opinion needed to close the deal, a city planner fidgeting with his color slides showing the technical stages of a proposed construction schedule—men and women whom no one in the room really knew.

All of this distancing and narrowing was summed up in the poignant remark of a young woman whom I overheard at the next table in a restaurant favored by young urban professionals. You know the kind of place, with butcher block tables set with fresh cut flowers, serving white wine and overpriced salads. The young woman wore conservative tweeds and granny glasses, her leather briefcase with brass fittings was close by, and the talk seemed mostly about convertible debentures. There was a moment, however, when she tried to explain to her friends why she was more interested in the homeless on the streets than she was in the bond market. She shrugged and laughed, "Oh, you can't change the way you are just because of what you do."

But when important parts of you are not acknowledged by others, you can become wary of asserting yourself in any matter where you have no proven competence. To do so is to risk failure, rejection, or just being considered a fool. I don't know whether risk aversion is the natural disposition of those who choose specialist careers, or whether it is an acquired habit of training and practice. I do know that I simply was no longer willing to let myself be vulnerable around others, which may explain why so many dinner parties with professional friends found each of us talking shop endlessly. Without an entrepreneur or an artist at the table, we were capable of putting an entire dinner party to sleep in what Jacques Barzun called "the dreary exchange of affidavits, which passes for conversation."[4]

After getting away from my professional life for a while, I realized that being professional was largely a state of mind in which I had set the terms of my own confinement. In deciding to leave that privileged but limiting sanctuary, no doubt I became vulnerable again, but I was enormously encouraged about my prospects as a human being. Subsequently, when I settled into an academic life and my professional story resumed, I kept a wary eye on myself. As a recovering professional, I couldn't do otherwise.[5]

You can begin by trying to discover the "personal" reasons of experts, not the "professional" ones I discussed earlier, for why they might be willing to meet you halfway. Many experts had personal reasons for entering a specialized field unrelated to the professional orientation they were subjected to in their graduate school training and ongoing guild membership. Talk to a specialist who has found an expert niche, and you may learn that originally she simply wanted to help people or correct injustices. She may have had a broader aim than what she has accepted as a specialist and may have entertained an alternative career that she put aside but did not totally reject.

You can only learn about these personal reasons if you take the time to try to know the whole person and not just what her expertise offers. For all you know, she may be suffering from burnout in her expert niche and would welcome a different kind of challenge. Another specialist may regret that his preoccupation with maintaining status in his field has denied him the chance to be involved in the neighborhood and community where he lives. Can you tap the unused potential of such people who remain ready to think and act outside their respective boxes? Imagine seeking out the software code developer to help brainstorm a problem arising from a community outreach project of your organization. Imagine giving the designer of financial derivatives a chance to evaluate proposed incentives for the cross-training of veteran employees. Imagine asking the highway traffic engineer to join a temporary group redesigning office space to promote more collaboration across the organization. The possibilities are unlimited when you start thinking outside your box, which limits you to using only their expertise. Finding professional reasons for them is still your first priority and theirs, but finding personal reasons, after getting to know more about each of them, may help you engage their other talents as well.

Some specialists, however, may not be comfortable in accepting your invitation and may very well resist. Their golden rule is "defer unto others as you would have them defer unto you." They know that specialization and the strict boundaries of work that it establishes keep the peace in an organization. Experts aren't expected to work out of title anymore than a shipping clerk is. That's someone else's job, and we all have been conditioned to think that without special training and experience, we probably cannot perform such a task anyway. But all of this accommodation misses the point. Of course, you're not going to ask experts to switch jobs for a day, a week, or a month. That would be silly and resisted anyway. There are, however, many opportunities to get their input on a problem, a proposal, some undertaking that could use fresh perspectives. They can give advice without feeling accountable, take a busman's holiday that may also give them fresh perspectives on their own specialized work, or, at least, the chance to exercise unused talents that means a great deal for personal reasons.

You may be also doing them a favor by engaging them in informal groups whose work broadens their understanding of how many things get done without being centered on expertise. To get an expert's mind out of his accustomed groove helps him understand what other gifts are needed to collaborate successfully with others. As I noted in Chapter 3, getting it right, which is often the work of specialists, still requires getting it accepted. What better way to develop interactive skills than being part of diverse groups where no one's expertise is a trump card to play?

Experts on the outside may resist your efforts to get to know them better, believing that it fouls up the professional detachment and objectivity they need to serve a client's interests. And there is some merit in that attitude. If professional specialists are too engaged with their clients, they may compromise the very reason their services were sought in the first place. But I would argue that to develop a working relationship with the specialist that acknowledges the whole person does not necessarily rob him of the objectivity that he thinks he needs to help you. Getting to know an expert beyond understanding what he does, and his knowing you beyond what he thinks you want, should only improve the outcome. It should certainly improve your relations and mutual trust in any collaborations that arise later. Whatever else it does for the expert, getting to know and trust him makes it easier for you to know and trust his expertise.

NORTHWEST HOSPITAL: In the following vignette, what would you do about the professional culture at Northwest Hospital, if you succeeded Sylvie Ferrara as its administrator?

The *Valley News* story reports that the total nursing hours per patient day at Northwest will decline if a new "microhospital" plan is put into place. Such a plan is the brainchild of Northwest's cost containment consultant, Paula LeClerc. The consultant's plan calls for breaking Northwest into newly administered microhospitals. Instead of having one clerk per patient and a number of senior administrators overseeing all that goes on at Northwest, a smaller number of admitting clerks would be assigned to each microhospital, where they would assume responsibility for six to eight patients and work as part of a team composed of a registered nurse and a technician. LeClerc calls them "care-pairs."

All care-pairs would go through a six-week retraining so that they could perform as "multiskilled practitioners" doing

80 to 90 percent of the pre- and postsurgical care. In addition, there would be a computer terminal in each patient's room with software prompts designed to assist the team on matters beyond their knowledge or control. LeClerc estimates that registered nurses (RNs) would spend more time with patients while still allowing for a reduction in the overall nursing staff. The *Valley News* story reported that certain unnamed doctors associated with Northwest have expressed their concern for the quality of care if there is less nursing supervision.

Sylvie Ferrara, the hospital administrator of Northwest, was not pleased with the *Valley News* story and assumes that there were a number of people at the hospital who could have been sources for the article. Ferrara already knew that Doris Leonard, chief of nursing, was very concerned about staffing levels available on each floor at night. The hospital has fewer RNs than five years ago and has hired more licensed practical nurses instead. There is a significant difference in their training in pharmacology, for example, which has alarmed some people at Northwest. Leonard has also told Ferrara that some of her staff are worried that a multiskilled practitioner trained at Northwest, but looking for employment elsewhere, might be unsuccessful because other facilities don't offer such a job description.

Ferrara has already invested a lot of time and resources in LeClerc's idea. What prompted her interest in the first place was the fear of Republic HealthCare, Inc., which has begun to buy up hospitals all over the greater metropolitan area. Republic's tactic is to court local doctors and sell them a stake in the facilities that Republic takes over. Ferrara knew that hospitals like Northwest might ultimately close down or be absorbed by giants like Republic if her cost structure could not compete with Republic's ability to get big discounts from insurers and medical suppliers.

Still, Ferrara had warned LeClerc that the professional culture and morale at Northwest were not very hospitable to putting professionals together in novel combinations and with less oversight. One ally physician confided to Ferrara that some of his colleagues didn't think she was "sufficiently deferential to Northwest's professional hierarchy."

LeClerc, however, had countered that Doris Leonard and even Northwest's doctors might see the advantages of changing the professional culture if it meant ultimately saving jobs and improving patient care. LeClerc thought that younger doctors, who have been trained in general and family practice, would more readily choose to affiliate with Northwest if it adopted a new patient-centered attitude.

The *Valley News* story clearly called for a response. At least, that is what the chair of Northwest's Board, Bowden Blair, wanted Sylvie Ferrara to consider. Blair opened the staff meeting convened for just that purpose. "Sylvie, you brought Ms. LeClerc into Northwest and she brought along her plan, which in turn has brought the hospital bad press. The fact of the matter is that there must be dissatisfaction among Northwest's employees or they wouldn't feel compelled to talk to reporters."

Ferrara looked pointedly at Leonard. "It so happens that decreasing revenues are forcing me to develop cost-cutting strategies if we are to maintain our independent viability."

Doris Leonard returned Ferrara's pointed glance with remarks of her own. "I'm sorry, Sylvie, but further reductions in the RN staff will cause a decrease in the quality of care and more bad press for sure."

In response, Ferrara shook her head and looking at no one in particular said quietly but firmly, "What we have to do is get staff support at every level for a plan that can deliver quality care for less cost. I have already told Doris that the microhospital plan does not necessarily mean fewer RNs. The plan is designed to thin out the administrative staff, not to affect the quality of care. If it works as Paula says it will, we will have established a niche that should arrest our decline."

Doris Leonard was not finished. "I really think that it is a mistake that Northwest's doctors are not represented here. How can we run a hospital and leave them out of such a crucial meeting? For all we know, they may have talked to the press out of some pique of their own."

Blair waved his hands as if asking for a timeout. "I understand what you all must be going through trying to stabilize things around here. But we have to pull together and present a united front with whatever plan seems to make the most sense." Looking at his watch, the chair seemed to want to escape, start the meeting over, or perhaps find a new administrator.

LeClerc, who had been looking out the window as if to maintain a critical distance from the family quarrel, decided to intervene. "May I suggest that if bad press was the reason for this meeting in the first place that you consider refocusing the public's attention on the positive aspects and plans of the hospital. I don't think you have a lot of time before Republic HealthCare steps in and makes the case that everyone will be better served if it takes over Northwest."

CHAPTER 5

Changing the Status Quo

The Status Quo

Your mobility from one organization to another is an asset when used to take a fresh look at the circumstances of each new workplace and to think about the changes you would make if you could. Obviously, if you are on assignment and not staying long, you may not think you have a reason or the time. Maybe so, but your assignment itself or its success may depend on your smarts to get the organization, or some part of it, to change how it goes about doing things.

Changing the status quo usually means redoing something that is already there or adding something that does not yet exist. The previous chapters in this book have been a way of preparing you for this critical chapter of organizational life, which usually comes after you understand how the real organization works and what others want, and you have managed to establish a credible reputation and to work productively with experts. Changing the status quo tests what you have learned about an organization and about your colleagues and what they have learned about you.

The status quo is policies, procedures, and rules prescribed by higher-ups mixed with routines and practices maintained by lower-downs; it is whatever governs the conduct and performance of most people in the organization. It does not mean that everyone is happy with the status quo, only that they have accepted it, more or less. The status quo is the very human construction of coordination and predictability that most people prefer in their organizational lives.

It makes little sense, therefore, to denigrate the status quo until you learn what virtues it has for those who maintain it. Their competence, organizational identity, and sense of membership may be tied up with preserving it rather than putting at risk what they know for something unfamiliar. As noted in Chapter 1, the customs of an organization may seem arbitrary to a newcomer who has not yet experienced their benefits. If you do your detective work and still think the status quo needs fixing, at least you can appreciate why it has its defenders.

You may find the hardest thing to do is gaining the acceptance of others in an organization without fully accepting their status quo. It is a fine line to walk. Prospectors can become quite adept at switching jobs when that seems necessary or desirable, but in any organization there is likely to be a cast of characters who are not as light on their feet. They don't share your preference for mobility or your talent as a quick learner wherever you land. You may be in a hurry but they are not, and they have lots of personal reasons for not changing the status quo. Their own particular self-interests may not be served, or based on their experience in the organization they may not trust those who have sought change before. They may simply misunderstand what change-makers are up to, or they may have a differing assessment of what changes are needed. There are always those who just want to be left alone, thank you, and don't like the prospect of change in any form.[1]

Assuming that you stay around long enough, by all means take the time to consider what needs changing in an organization before you become a captive of its status quo and are no longer willing to see it as a problem. Anyone who stays in one place long enough is inclined to defend the status quo as a way of defending himself from those who come along and are critical of the organization's performance and, indirectly, his own performance. The longer you put up with the status quo, like it or not, the more implicated you become as one of those who presumably want to maintain it. Others may conclude that you are part of the problem, not part of the solution. Try to deal with the problems you find before being tempted to deny their existence. One reason people move on to a new organization is that they give up on their current organization and give up on themselves to change its status quo. They lose the interest or capacity to be a change-maker. The conditions are no longer favorable, their credibility as a change-maker is suspect, and those few who looked to them for help have started to drift away.

Changing the status quo in timely and effective ways, however, is very difficult work. If you think the status quo is a problem, trying to change it may be an even bigger problem. Consider the subsections of this chapter as stages you move through from a status quo in an organization to something better. It does not happen overnight.

You first have to think hard about the changes you want. Perhaps it is more productivity in a particular unit, or better communication and consultation across departments, something that is not going to happen unless you help make it happen. Your preparation should include learning about any earlier attempts that have failed and why. Chapter 1 called for such detective work to avoid an awkward start of seeking a change that you think is new to the organization, only to find out that it has already been proposed or tried. It is very common for naysayers in an organization to be dismissive of any renewed effort, citing previous attempts as reason enough to resist a new one. Past failures, however, do not prevent you from trying again. The point is to acknowledge past efforts, to learn from them, and to be prepared to explain why your effort can succeed where others have not.

Even more important than knowing what changes you want is mobilizing support for them. Your individual-centered talent for moving on and getting ahead does not help you much here unless you know how to get your organization-centered colleagues to help you. Without them, you can always change jobs, but you can't do much about changing the organization. It takes the willing cooperation of *enough others,* whether that turns out to be two or two hundred, and such cooperation may be very hard to mobilize. Think of change not just as what you want to do but what people you need to get that done. The status quo is lodged in their resistance, indifference, or wait-and-see attitude.

THE STATUS QUO IN BROOKDALE COUNTY: | Consider
what you would make of the following conversation concerning the status quo in your department and Brookdale County.
You are the new county commissioner of the general services department, and part of a new county administration.

The new Brookdale County executive, Jo Burke, has just won a resounding victory over a Republican regime that ruled the county for sixteen years, and she did it with the help of a revitalized county Democratic party under the leadership of an auto-parts dealer, Mitch Pesiri.

Just this morning you learned that Pesiri wants to continue a longstanding practice of the party in power of dividing insurance commissions among brokers in the county as an exercise in party patronage. Brenda James, the veteran risk manager in your department, told you all about it over a morning cup of coffee.

"Mitch Pesiri wasted no time." Brenda laughed. "He came into my office yesterday afternoon and told me that from now on the Simmons Agency will handle all county insurance business. Archie Simmons is an old friend of Pesiri and the party. Simmons is also one of the biggest and best insurance agencies in the county. Under the Republicans, Archie was cut out of the action. Most of the business went to Prendergast & Sons."

You interrupted Brenda. "But what is the point of your job if the county uses outside insurance brokers?"

"Oh, I still make most of the decisions," Brenda replied, "where we self-insure, what limits to carry, deductibles, et cetera. The outside agency administers the routine claims to keep my staff costs down. We pay the insurance premiums to Simmons, who then renews the coverage or secures coverage from some other reputable insurance carrier. Simmons keeps a percentage of the premium as his commission and forwards the net premium to the carrier."

"Brenda, I still don't understand your point. Pesiri chooses the broker who, you say, earns the commission. So?"

Brenda laughed again. "But then Pesiri reenters the picture. He will go to Simmons, just as the Republican County leader used to pay an annual call on Prendergast, and submit a list of local brokers who are to share in 25 percent of the commissions that Simmons has earned. Pesiri's list of brokers to be paid accomplishes two purposes. First, the brokers are less likely to squawk that Simmons got the major business if they are cut in on part of the action. Second, they are more likely to work for the party or buy a table at the annual party dinner if they want to be on Pesiri's list."

Brenda is a longtime employee of the department and considered a first-class civil servant. You were tempted to ask why she seemed so indifferent to the commission sharing but instead suggested that the matter be discussed with Jo Burke.

"But Ms. Burke knows about it," Brenda declared. "Pesiri told me so. Do you think I take my cue from a party boss? You should understand something, Commissioner. Those commissions used to belong to Prendergast. At renewal time, they now will go to Archie Simmons. What those gentlemen do with them is none of my business. As long as the county gets good service from the primary broker, that's all that counts with me."

As you stared at your shoes, Brenda went on. "And you have to understand something else, Commissioner. The insurance carriers want to pay the commissions. That's the 'independent agency system.' The carriers don't care what Simmons does with the commissions. As far as the insurance companies are concerned, commissions keep the agency system alive and that's good for the insurance business."

You start to turn over some questions in your mind. If Simmons shares his commission with brokers who do nothing to earn it, is it an unnecessary cost to the public, or is it just a business expense of Simmons? Should the county negotiate lower commissions with insurance carriers if Simmons is willing to give away 25 percent of his commissions to brokers on Pesiri's list, or should the county do away with brokers altogether?

When you pose these questions to Brenda James she gives you the case history of what the government in an adjoining state went through when it tried to do away with the practice of commission sharing.

"After our neighboring state decided to negotiate all insurance policies directly with the carriers on a net basis, with no commission payable to brokers, the major insurance carriers balked. The carriers advised the state that unless it agreed to designate brokers for the carriers' insurance policies, they would not do business with the state. The carriers said they were under pressure from the Insurance Agents Association whose members account for 99.9 percent of the carriers' business. Can you believe it, Commissioner? Our neighboring state then found itself facing a rise in its insurance costs because the most favorable rates had usually come from those carriers who accept insurance placements through the independent agency system."

You know that you owe Jo Burke a visit. But what exactly is it that you want to tell her?

Precipitating Events

Change is rarely something that you can conceive, initiate, and implement in one continuous swing like the polished fairway swing of a good golfer. You rarely have sufficient control in an organization to bring about change on your terms and with the sure timing that such control implies. Change-making is normally more opportunistic than that, and, besides, control by itself does not ensure that change will be readily accepted and secured. Remember you need the willing cooperation of others to make it work, and that takes more than just throwing your weight around.

Since you are not likely to be in control, you should be prepared to take advantage of events that are beyond your control. This is the opportunistic dimension of changing the status quo, knowing how to use what I call a "precipitating event" to advance your cause in an organization. The precipitating event may be an unfavorable audit report, a whistleblower generating a bad press story, the unexpected termination of a big funding grant, a proposed merger with another organization, a new CEO—whatever is significant enough to get the organization's full attention.

In many cases, those who seek change do not so much plan its introduction as respond to events that permit it. This is not as wobbly a strategy as it sounds. Real change in an organization may not be possible unless some precipitating event forces those who have ignored or resisted change to reconsider their options. Such an event can rattle an organization and temporarily unsettle or disarm those who are guardians of the status quo. When we say "things will never be the same," our reference is often to events beyond our control that we think will permanently alter how "things" are done. New circumstances threaten the organization and the status quo is just no longer tenable.

A precipitating event confronting an organization offers you the opportunity to make a plausible connection between the changes you want and the abnormal conditions that destabilize the status quo. You were not the first to rock the boat, but now that it is rocking, you can put your oar in, too. You are probably not the only one who seeks to take advantage of the situation. Recall the City

Electric vignette in Chapter 3 when the threat of layoffs and a takeover, hostile or otherwise, led certain key players at the utility to reconsider the "balanced workforce plan" of affirmative action.

If a precipitating event doesn't get people's attention immediately, the talk of a crisis will. Such an escalation of the rhetoric creates an expectation that change is necessary and unavoidable, and it is not unheard for higher-ups to manufacture a crisis by the language they use at meetings, in memos, or with interested players outside the organization. Once a "crisis" is declared and accepted as a credible threat, it becomes easier to make personnel changes, reallocate budget resources, and reform organizational practices, all of which are more difficult to do without the rationale of a crisis.

Consider any crisis in an organization as a potentially favorable condition whether it feeds on the alarm that some event precipitates or is part of a deliberate strategy to foster change. It may well be beyond your control to end the crisis, but see it as an opening and use it as a wedge to further your effort. Just be sure you also make clear to your colleagues and higher-ups how your proposal can help them address the crisis. Their consuming interest will be the crisis, not your proposal.

If you get a chance to do some crisis framing yourself, try to make it a good fit with your talents. You would obviously prefer to be a key player and not just a messenger. Crisis framing is much like the problem framing that I discussed in Chapter 3, when players choose frames that reflect their own training, organizational role, or personal values. I recall my time on the board of the New York Metropolitan Transportation Authority in the 1980s when two different chairmen, Dick Ravitch and his successor, Bob Kiley, each defined that agency's crisis in terms that best suited their respective talents. Ravitch talked of a "financing crisis," which he set about solving by raising new capital funds from the state legislature and from creating new debt instruments that appealed to private capital markets. It so happened that Ravitch's talent was in capital finance. Bob Kiley, a transit executive from Boston, understandably talked of an "operations crisis," which he set about solving by recruiting talented outsiders to shake up the bus and subway bureaucracies and by pursuing new strategies of fleet maintenance.

It is likely that the crisis in an organization is not of your making but, rather, is framed by someone else or triggered by a precipitating event over which no one in the organization has control. Whatever the source, the currency of change proposals becomes highly valued. At the time of New York City's fiscal crisis in the late 1970s, our new administration was beleaguered and overwhelmed in City Hall, getting unsolicited help from all corners—new appointees, incumbent officials, and interested outsiders pressing a slew of their proposals for change. I did not begrudge such lobbying; it was a time of enormous flux in how the city's government went about its business. There was no way that a new administration could have all the answers, and various would-be players saw a chance to advance their ideas—fiscal, financial, and operational. A few of the change proposals were brilliantly conceived, others were hopelessly muddled, and many bore little relation to the crisis but were reforms that our creditors—the bondholders, private capital markets, state and federal governments—might welcome. We greeted the best ideas of these opportunists with opportunism of our own. Long-standing accounting practices were changed, contracts renegotiated, capital projects set aside, and new undertakings encouraged, some of which had little directly to do with the fiscal crisis itself.

Ed Koch was like a new general in an old war zone. Parachuted into the front lines, the newly elected mayor had five stars on his helmet, but he had not been tested in combat. Looking out from their command posts, banking, business, and labor leaders saluted the five stars but immediately began to test his campaign pledge to restore investor confidence in New York City. The fiscal crisis also opened the door to their change agendas. I recall attending a meeting of the Business-Labor Working Group, where I made it clear, on behalf of the new administration, that many of their major, but controversial, economic development projects requiring governmental action would go forward—a site for a proposed convention center, the resuscitation of Battery Park City, and plans for a riverfront Westway. And when certain leaders of the real estate industry asked for new rent policies that would stimulate the private housing market, the mayor told me that we might have to put an end to residential rent controls. Talk about change! As it turned out, no new rent policies saw the light of day, but internal planning for what would have been a revolution did go on in my office for almost a year.

> **THE DEPARTMENT OF MOTOR VEHICLES (DMV):** The DMV is rarely in the public limelight, but now the state's new governor, Lulu Camenetti, needs to make good on her campaign pledge to run a "customer friendly" government. With the state in terrible fiscal shape, Camenetti has to focus on cutting costs, lowering taxes, and putting the customer-citizen first. So her staff, which you have recently joined, is looking at how to improve the performance of every state agency, and you have been assigned to wrestle with the long-standing complaints about DMV's "serpentine lines" and "discourteous staff."
>
> You have learned that the attitude problem at DMV is exacerbated by the number of DMV locations around the state that are housed in county clerks' offices and staffed by county employees who act as agents for DMV but are not state employees. This arrangement exists because it saves the

state a lot of money and lets local political leaders use their patronage powers without DMV interference.

The current DMV deputy commissioner, Fran Medwick, a favorite of the county clerks around the state, has made it known that her long-standing political friendship with the new governor (Medwick befriended Camenetti countless times as Lulu made a name for herself as a public-interest lawyer) will help maintain her dominance in the department. In fact, she fully expects to be promoted to commissioner "if the governor wants help in dealing with key state legislators and the county clerks to weather the state's fiscal crisis."

Just yesterday, however, someone suggested that the governor appoint new blood at DMV and recommended Jan Powers to be its new commissioner. Powers has worked as a consultant with various jurisdictions, helping state and local governments reinvent themselves—test-marketing self-service computerized terminals in California shopping malls, where citizens can carry out a variety of transactions (taxes, hunting and fishing permits, voter registration), running customer surveys for Michigan court systems and Illinois police departments, and establishing customer (resident) councils in public housing projects throughout the country.

When you went to the governor's private office this morning to brief her on the DMV, she looked uneasy. For Camenetti, one big issue was money. You already knew that the current draft of the next fiscal year's budget was looking for a 5 percent cut from every state agency. In addition, the governors' Office of Management and Budget was asking for a 20 percent hike in driver and registration fees at DMV, one of thirty-two revenue measures to close the big state deficit.

She told you that Medwick has made clear that the DMV will
never get the attention of the county clerks' employees or
improve their attitude toward the public unless the state
makes a substantial investment in training programs. "Fran
has assured me," the governor noted, "that she can go out
and collect some political IOUs from the county clerks so that
they put some of their own county money into such a project." Then Camenetti looked at you. "Will all this buy a
change in attitude toward the public?"

Do you think the state's fiscal crisis can help sell Powers
to the governor, or is Medwick the better choice?

When a precipitating event or a looming crisis offers you the
opportunity to get attention paid to changes you want, it still may
take a while before people are ready to let go of their status quo.
"Sometimes things have to get worse before they can get better."
Why do we say that? The premise is that we have to *experience* a
problem before we are ready to do something about it. In our private lives, an energy crisis may not get us to change our conserva-
tion habits until there are brownouts or blackouts or exorbitant
gas prices. In the 1970s, motorists didn't buy fuel-efficient cars
until their gas guzzlers busted their monthly budgets or too often
put them in long lines at the gas pump.[2] They had to experience
the problem, not just read or hear about it. As things got worse,
people realized that things couldn't get better until they changed
the status quo.

So it can take time in an organization before conditions
become ripe enough for change. A precipitating event and the talk
of an internal crisis may alert everyone, but your colleagues may
not appreciate what it means for their daily work lives. There is a
big difference between listening to productivity consultants and

seeing actual layoffs on their floor, between hearing about others' computer problems and having their hard drive crash, or between fielding complaints about miscommunication among departments and losing an important contract for failing to meet a RFP deadline. Individual worries, nagging concerns, and gripes in the grapevine often fall short of being an organization's problem until people personally experience the pain of what it means and there are real consequences to live with. "Things get worse" when their best friend gets a pink slip on Friday, or they have to spend long nights rebuilding a database, or they lose a much-needed bonus because of interdepartmental snafus. When they exchange and share these individual experiences, there is the chance that things can get better, because the organization as a social organism now feels the pain, too.

Now obviously you don't want to be a party to making things worse in an organization in order to get people's serious attention, but you should be on the lookout for ways that potential allies can personally experience what you have told them needs fixing. I can tell my dean about the problem of getting various colleagues to cooperate in revising our curriculum, but if I convince him to sit in on one of our dysfunctional meetings, his experience brings alive my complaint. I can tell my colleagues that some students may consider transferring or dropping out until we can get our curriculum act together, but if I can arrange for them to meet with these students, such conversations bring home an urgency about enrollments and the curriculum.

The status quo is very hard to budge by merely imploring others to change it. People nod their heads but have lots of other things to do. So think of ways not only to help colleagues and higher-ups experience the problem, but also to experience the change you want. For example, if poor communication is the status quo and no remedies seem to be in the offing, take it upon yourself to be an exemplar of how good communication can work. Make the effort to share information beyond the need-to-know category of colleagues. Let those not in the loop experience what it means to be included. Your example by itself will not change the status quo, but it may help to show how things could improve if enough others joined you in enlarging the circle. Your colleagues may say, "Why can't others communicate around here like you do?" Wouldn't that be nice?

Setting an example doesn't have to come with a lot of preaching and teaching. Critical talk and talk of change may even be counterproductive if people are not yet ready to listen or to act. They may see you as an unschooled newcomer or a grump who hasn't yet found a secure niche like they have. What may be more effective is getting them to appreciate the difference of how you do certain things in the organization. Finding ways for them to experience both the downside of what bothers you and the upside of what can take its place may be necessary preliminaries before you can get their help to change the status quo.

Finding Allies

Whatever event or crisis puts an organization in motion, don't be misled by the seeming appearance of people ready to accept a change of the status quo. Change is usually threatening and disconcerting, and there are those who do nothing more than talk about change using a vocabulary of good intentions. Their e-mails and meetings are laced with verbs of action, "undertake" and "implement" being favorites, which often promote only the illusion of change as they try to go about their organizational business as usual. They have no intention of walking their talk. What can make real change so devilishly hard is the passive resistance of those who do not announce their opposition to change but who do as little as possible to accommodate it.

These are certainly not the people you should seek out as allies. They will continue to limit their role in the organization to those tasks for which they are trained and hired. They will continue to defend their designated place, perform their assigned tasks, and assume that others will do the same. When change is pressed on them, their adjustment is slow, and retaining the security of a designated place in the organization becomes even more important. They are not likely to put the interests of the organization or your efforts at change above their own. Change may put too much at risk for them.

So who can you count on? One challenge for anyone on the side of change is finding those who have both the talent and a reason for promoting it, sometimes referred to as "change agents." No one is usually hired to be a change agent. A change agent acts as a catalyst, helping to achieve a desired result without altering his or her own position. Whether a change agent is an inside player or an outside consultant, the role is temporary. Look around; you may be the only one available.

A few months after I left City Hall, a remark of a former colleague made me realize that my personal presence was not so much missed as was the role I had played.

"Brown," he told me, "I never quite knew what you did when you were here, but now that you're gone, I think I know."

My temporary role, in helping to promote a number of personnel and policy changes in a new administration, was born of necessity. It came unannounced. I functioned with what some described as a low profile. Like footprints, whatever impression my role made could only be seen after my departure. Even I had no name for the role until my colleague's remark confirmed its absence.

CHANGE AGENTS: In the following vignette, who would make the best change agent?

The deputy commissioner greeted you at the Department of Investigation's reception desk and ushered you to the large corner office that was now yours as the department's new commissioner. Daniel Cobb was a blunt and forceful person with staff, with strangers, and even with his new boss.

"I've had the honor to serve three commissioners, and I'm sure I can serve my fourth with distinction, and that goes for all the staff too—we're professionals."

It had been rumored, however, that Cobb, who was generally well liked by the staff, might soon retire, leading an exodus of veterans from the department. Would a new inexperienced staff be sufficient for what was expected of your department? Would the central Office of Management and Budget pursue its usual tactic of "delay and save" before approving critical new hires?

Cobb raised with you the issue of a revised salary plan for the department that had been pending for nine months. Cobb explained that department employees not covered by collective bargaining were still waiting for new salary range levels to be established. Cobb insisted that the salary question be addressed if you expected more productivity from the staff.

Your meeting with Cobb was followed by a conversation with the department's chief counsel, Cris Calhoun. Calhoun was a bright and ambitious woman who had made it known that she wanted Cobb's job when he left. She did not hide her contempt for your predecessor, who failed to challenge Cobb's tight hold on the staff. You had heard that Calhoun's aggressive style made it easy for Cobb to isolate her from his conservative followers, but she still hoped to find a commissioner who would be the indispensable ally she needed to break Cobb's grip on the department.

Later that day you went to lunch with Tony Alger, the young aide that the mayor said he could make available to you on a temporary basis. You briefed Alger on your conversations of that morning with Cobb and Calhoun. Alger's advice was that you should hire new personnel quickly. You could not afford to wait for Cobb and his "bureaucrats" to decide whether to "put out" for you or take their pensions and go. Alger was sure he could help loosen Cobb's hold on the agency and force his retirement, if that's what you wanted.

From the lunch with Alger, you crossed the street to City Hall and met with Charles Abrams, the department's chief accountant. Abrams was a civil servant like Cobb and Calhoun but had developed a tax practice on his own time that had given him financial independence. His wife had wanted him to give up the department job, but he had stayed on in order to groom one of his young investigative accountants as a successor. Abrams offered no criticism of Cobb or Calhoun, although he did find it necessary from time to time to assume the role of peacemaker between them. The salary plan had been a particular bone of contention. Abrams admitted, though, that his influence on Cobb was episodic and not continuous.

Change agents are hard to find, but you need allies from the get-go. Whom can you get to be part of a coalition? A coalition is usually a temporary grouping of interested parties who share a common goal. Seek out those who stand to gain from the change you want to introduce. Your job is not just to explain why the change makes sense for the organization but also why the change makes sense for each of them as well. They may want the change for very different reasons, using you in much the same way as you use a precipitating event or crisis. They can be good opportunists, too.

When you think about building a coalition, however, you may want it only as a construct in your mind, not as an identifiable group to others in the organization, at least not at first. Such visibility could be counterproductive, a kind of us-against-them look that you probably don't want, and your allies might not want any part of either. Your allies may not even like each other very much and have other issues that divide them. Coalition building does not have to include holding conspiratorial meetings or sharing surreptitious e-mails. Your job is to accommodate your allies' divergent interests by doing favors, asking favors, and keeping each of them informed of what progress is being made.

Your allies should not complicate your task so much that it's not worth accommodating them. Their numbers don't count so much as your knowing that they have their own good reasons for joining you. Numbers come later when you try to bring everyone else along. Remember the envelope game that I described in Chapter 2, in which it is very difficult to get timely cooperation from a large group. It is important that the few allies you can find don't play the same tentative game. Coalitions work best when each temporary member extends his or her unconditional cooperation. At some point, you may suffer some defections among your allies, but if you don't think you can count on them from the outset, don't bother including them.

Leaving players out of your coalition who should be included is as bad as including those who should probably be left out. As discussed in Chapter 1, figure out the power relations for the particular change you want. Who can stymie your effort? If you want to change the status quo, are there particular people whom you absolutely need on your side? They may be key associates of yours who are entitled to know what you're up to. You don't want to jeopardize your ongoing relationships by leaving them in the dark. There may be others who deserve a heads up, too. Many people's opinions will be shaped not by what they think of your change effort but how you treat them as you pursue it. If all this sounds like politics, know that it is just that. It is said that experts seek data, but politicians seek allies. If talk about politics bothers you or others, don't use the term, but find your allies and build your coalition.

CACTUS CORP.: Try "Horse Trading at Cactus Corp." as a way of limbering up your mind about coalitions.

The five disreputable owners of Cactus Corp. have fallen out over whether Cactus should move its operations offshore to avoid U.S. taxes or pay a high-powered lobbyist to get tax loophole legislation passed that would accomplish the same purpose. Either course of action requires the approval of both the directors and the stockholders.

Arson is for the offshore option. Bandit is for the loophole option. Cutthroat, Dirty, and Ex-Con are on the fence, and, since there is no honor among thieves, their votes are for sale, but not their shares. Arson owns 5 million shares, Bandit owns 4 million shares, Cutthroat owns 3 million shares, Dirty owns 2 million shares, and Ex-Con owns 1 million shares.

At their stockholder meetings, decisions are made by a majority vote of the shares. The same five characters also make up the board of directors, whose decisions are also decided by a majority vote of the directors. As a minimum, whom does Arson need in his coalition? As a minimum, whom does Bandit need in his coalition? Who has disproportionate leverage (a "swing" vote) as a stockholder? As a director?

Assume for the moment that you find your allies, but a higher-up turns a deaf ear or in other ways lets you know that he is not prepared to support your effort. One precipitating event of your own making might be the threat of moving on. I do not recommend it as a tactic for the fainthearted, or if you have good reason to remain in the organization with or without the changes that you think would be beneficial. But if your credibility with allies or other colleagues is at stake because the organization's hierarchy has left you hanging, the threat of moving on may be a critical or necessary step to consider. It can be part of any prospector's repertoire.

The threat should be made in private so that the higher-up can weigh what to do without appearing to be the loser. If retaining your talent counts more than the disputed change in question, then the change may be embraced in order to keep its advocate. You should try to weigh those concerns in advance, to see what you would do if you were in his shoes. If you have established a reputation for "walking your talk," as discussed in Chapter 2, the threat may well succeed. If it does not prove successful, then your status with colleagues and your standing with higher-ups may become so tenuous that you will want to move on. In such a circumstance, it probably makes sense to leave without making further waves, in order to retain your marketability with future employers. In any event, try to explain to your allies, who remain in the organization or who are associated with it, what was at stake, at least for you. I hope your change efforts don't take you on such a wild ride, but you are the only one who knows how far you are prepared to go.

Finding Enough Others

What is the difference between finding allies and finding enough others? Allies work with you; enough others is the number that you need in order to succeed. See your lift off in two stages: the booster section of allies getting your change off the launching pad; enough others getting it into orbit. There is no way I can estimate how many others you need to get your change accepted and practiced in an organization. You probably won't have a clear read on that number either, but knowing in advance how many you need is not the point. Knowing that you need enough others is.[3]

A threshold can be reached without knowing exactly where it is. If this all seems a bit mysterious, let me give you some examples from your daily life that should reassure you that finding enough others is a goal you can reach without being able to predict in advance what its number should be. There you are, trying to cross the street on a "walk" light, but cars keep turning right into your crosswalk, preventing you from doing so. How many other pedestrians does it take to stop the cars and give your platoon a chance to cross? You're driving along on an unfamiliar stretch of interstate and everyone is exceeding the speed limit with no seeming fear of being pulled over by a police cruiser. How many cars did it take to set the "conventional speed" on that part of the highway? At the end of a virtuoso performance of a favorite Beethoven symphony, some members of the concert audience get up and applaud to express their appreciation. How many concertgoers does it take to produce a standing ovation throughout the hall? Enough others in these three instances is not a matter of counting noses. There are enough others when the traffic stops and lets you cross, when the police cruisers concede that the conventional speed is reasonable under the circumstances, and when those who might otherwise stay in their seats rise to join those applauding the orchestra's performance.

If I want to improve the communication among those working in my organization, I might think that enough others is persuading higher-ups to use what authority they have to prescribe new protocols for how people use e-mail, share new information, send out meeting agendas, interact at those meetings, advise students, brief visitors, and so on. If I believe, however, that such higher-ups are too often ignored or questioned, then enough others is a different set of players. Perhaps it is the program chairs (the graduate school is divided into five specialized degree programs) who could take the initiative to improve communication and make better use of the limited resources their programs share. If the full-time faculty or staff is the larger cohort needed, then my threshold of enough others is raised significantly. Keep in mind that I'm not talking about an ideal number but a doable number—whom does it take to get my organization's attention and to create the likelihood that the status quo can be changed?

THE CHANGE GAME: The one-round envelope game in Chapter 2 did not offer very good prospects for success. Now let me tell you how the game can be played as a multiround exercise similar to the stages that a change effort may go through before eventually succeeding or failing to take hold in an organization. I call it the "change game," and this is how I structure it for fifteen or more players.

1. A player gets the game under way by proposing a specific change of the status quo in an organization or community shared by all the other players. For the proposal to be admitted into the game, it must impose an effort cost on every player who supports the change. For example, proposing to work on weekends to garner more service contracts would be admitted. Proposing an end-of-the-year bonus pool would not. For each round of a game, a player has two choices, to cooperate (thumbs up) or not (thumbs down). Sound familiar?

2. I determine how many cooperators (C) are needed and how many rounds (R) are allowed, but I don't disclose either number to the players. My rule of thumb is: the more effort cost that I think is needed for a proposed change to succeed, the larger the number of cooperators (C) that is required, but a larger number of rounds (R) is allowed. I put the numbers for (C) and (R) on a board out of their view.

3. For each round, players choose to cooperate or not by a show of thumbs with eyes closed in lieu of secret ballots, which is too time consuming. I count the thumbs and announce how many cooperated and how many did not in the round. A player's choices from round to round depend on (a) how much the player values the proposed change and (b) how much the player is influenced by what others chose to do in the previous round. No communication among the players is allowed—that's what makes it a game.

4. Play continues until the predetermined (C) is reached or the predetermined (R) ends a game. For each game played, a player is credited with two points when (C) is reached within (R). A player is debited one point for every round in which she or he cooperates when (C) is not reached within (R). This penalty represents the unrewarded effort cost to the player.

5. After a number of games, play ends and players anonymously put their total point scores on cards and give them to me. I then put all the individual scores on a board for them to see.

> Most players' net scores will be in negative territory, indicating the personal cost associated with a change effort, successful or not. When players argue that it doesn't pay to cooperate if a negative score is all they can get, I tell them a positive score is all but impossible. In this game, there is no reward without an effort cost. That is why some kinds of change are hard to achieve.

Many people in an organization probably think of themselves as marginal. When change is introduced, they may not welcome it and are likely either to resist or wait and see. Don't become discouraged with the hangers-back. Use their reluctance to get others to step forward, telling them how much their participation is needed. If you can single them out for attention and persuade them that their help is crucial for enlisting others' cooperation, you may be able to get them off the fence, which eventually brings along enough others to tip the organization in favor of the change. Remember, however, that at best they are only conditional cooperators and are likely to drop out if not enough others go along eventually, too. So you not only want to engage them but keep them engaged. For this they need feedback about what others are doing. Conditional cooperators depend on feedback to help them adjust their effort level. The brave ones make an effort to incorporate the change, until too many others don't. The cautious ones hang back, waiting for evidence that the change has a chance to succeed. For both kinds of colleagues, positive feedback helps to sustain the brave and draw in the cautious.

From the outset, the change may be visible and reinforcing, the productivity boost that comes when people handle more matters in the same amount of time, or the improvement in communication across departments helping the organization respond better to customer requests and deadlines. But the change may be less visible, and here is where you can help with feedback that encourages those who might otherwise sit on the sidelines. For example, I made a point of e-mailing members of a working group that higher-ups were following with great interest and enthusiasm the group's progress in developing new elective courses. For some of those in the group who were laggards, I found that their output increased. For those already taking the lead, their work also improved, knowing that our group was getting attention. My feedback helped to fill some information gaps and to overcome some lingering doubts that the eventual products of our working group would be taken seriously.

I am even prone to a little exaggeration to make people feel better about the changes that they are trying to put in place. If my car is stuck in a snowbank, I have to persuade passersby that their cooperation in rocking and pushing the car is absolutely necessary. I will certainly be tempted to exaggerate the prospects of their success. This would not be deliberate deception, but only a kind of unexamined optimism that draws them into the organized effort. If I am convinced that my car is hopelessly stuck, it does little good to recruit their help. We won't succeed. If, however, I really don't know how many it will take, but I am sure that enough of us can manage to free the car from the snowbank, then it is to my advantage and probably to those who stopped to help, that each of them thinks that they make a critical difference. What any change effort must do is get its car rocking with the gift of optimism.[4]

The "change game" that I described earlier has an additional dimension when players consider their choices as members of a group. Then they are more likely to do what they think is expected of them as members. It is harder to hang back once the group has decided to cooperate. In all likelihood, you have little influence on your colleagues' ties to their respective units or departments and their sense of membership in one subculture or another. But if you have done your detective work to discover that such group identities exist, then seek out those whose opinion or example does have influence within their group. Your job is to keep them in the loop about what progress is being made and what is at stake for the organization. The opinions of unofficial leaders can be sufficiently persuasive or contagious to get others to go along with the change. Such leaders may prove to be valuable allies in prompting cooperation from members of their group whose ties are reason enough to support the change regardless of what each may think individually about its merits.

The experts, whose talents you need but whose work you cannot direct, may not be swayed, like other subgroups, by their member bonds. More than most they think for themselves and are not likely to be impressed by what others are doing to accommodate the change. They will probably evaluate any change on the basis of how it impacts their work, not its consequence for the organization as such. You will have to go out of your way to put yourself in their shoes to find reasons why a particular change can help them. It may even be an opportunity to engage their personal interests and talents as discussed in Chapter 4, which go beyond the bounds of their expertise but relate well to what you are trying to do in the organization.

As you read this section, I suspect that one of your reactions may be, "Hey, in my organization most people do what they're told. You make change sound like a blood donor campaign, where everyone has a choice whether to cooperate or not."

You're both right and wrong, right that change may be delivered with the authority of higher-ups, but wrong that change succeeds on those terms. For change to work, it takes the willing cooperation of enough others. What makes changing the status quo such difficult work for anyone is that policy pronouncements, organizational restructuring, and strategic plans do not by themselves produce actual change. Most changes require putting aside old ways of doing things and making a genuine effort to put new ways of doing things in place. It requires more than silent consent. Like an invading army, change and its agents can occupy the territory but find it difficult to govern. For the changes that really matter in an organization and are likely to really matter to you, authority alone is not enough. Enough others willing to cooperate is.

LITTER CITY: You are the new city manager of "Litter City." The small city of l00,000 has an overwhelming problem of litter. As more of it piles up and blows about, it is hard to know where it comes from and who is responsible for it. As more litter has accumulated, people seem to be more careless, thinking that one more beer can or fast food bag won't make much of a difference. Hardly anyone picks up after others anymore. There is just too much of the stuff.

Earlier this year Litter City was shocked by the announcement that a major service industry in town is seriously thinking of relocating its business elsewhere, which would mean the loss of more than 700 jobs. The CEO has found it hard to attract new managers to live in Litter City. A group of citizens responded with a call to arms, "Litter City has to clean up its act." A citywide meeting of citizens was held, but there was a disappointing turnout. The mayor, however, did attend, and she was bombarded with questions. She had very few answers. Nothing has worked. Anti-litter posters have been torn down, litter barrels stolen, the city budget squeezed, and a bond issue for more sanitation trucks defeated.

Nonetheless, a concerned citizens group appealed to everyone through local newspaper advertisements and letters to clean up their yard from back fence to front curb, each day and every day. The group asked store owners to do the same and asked the sanitation department to take care of those places that were left over. The reaction was not only disappointing but unsettling. Angry landlords accused tenants of being responsible for the mess around their buildings. Storeowners blamed customers. Many homeowners considered the cleanup overwhelming and asked that City Hall do it. Many protested that the litter on their lots came from somewhere else, and it wasn't fair to be saddled with cleaning up what other people were responsible for. Some homeowners, in fact, laboriously cleaned up their properties but soon became discouraged when their neighbors didn't.

When word got around that City Hall might raise taxes to pay for more sanitation workers if the voluntary cleanup didn't work, some homeowners organized and threatened to defeat anyone at the next election who sponsored such a measure. One man wrote a letter to the local newspaper telling everybody why he wanted to leave Litter City for good. "I don't want to spend the rest of my life picking up litter and worrying about whether my neighbors are doing the same. The aggravation isn't worth it!"[5]

Now what would you do?

Securing Change

Think of changes in an organization where you have worked before. New ways of doing things were put in place after some disruption and turmoil in the organization. At the outset, they were fragile and not expected to survive. There was confusion and resistance. As time went on, however, older employees accepted them or retired, and new employees assumed such practices were routine and expected. The status quo shifted, and eventually fewer people recalled or even knew how tenuous such practices once were. If you were to go back to your former workplace and someone said: "That's the way we do things around here," you could be sure that the changes are secure.[6]

Your change effort in any organization may take a similar path. Don't assume that initial or gradual acceptance guarantees lasting success. If it were that easy, why would I describe the status quo as so difficult to overcome? I have seen too many change-makers who use their guile and talent to introduce change and then assume that their work is mostly done. They have lavished their attention on the uphill struggle to change people's minds and habits and then turned away to other matters, only to find later that the ball has rolled back down the hill.

The status quo or its equivalent can reassert itself when those who opposed the change or who hung back find themselves in new positions of responsibility or with new allies of their own. They do not so much counterattack as de-emphasize or rework the change so that it hardly resembles what was intended to happen. A familiar example is when a committee tries to "clarify" a change. The result is a revised office procedure or organization policy with so many new amendments or badly written provisions that it makes a muddle of what was originally a model of clarity. Or someone who succeeds to the change-maker's position does not agree with what has been done and through neglect simply lets the progress made get lost as new agendas are developed. An equally problematic outcome is when a change effort leads to consequences that the change-maker did not contemplate or prepare for. There are often by-products or unintended consequences, both good and bad.[7]

At some point you should ask yourself an important hypothetical question: "If I were to leave the organization tomorrow, would the change that I have engineered survive me?" Given your likely mobility, this may not be so hypothetical. Whatever stage your career is in and however confident you are of your change effort succeeding, the question is an important reality check. If you are on the move, you don't want your hard work to go for naught, and you may need to take extra precautions so that the changes that take hold in the organization do not get put aside after you're gone.

Ask yourself the further question: "Whom do I need to secure the change if I am not around anymore?" You can become so engaged with your change-making that you can forget that most other people in the organization don't know that much about what you have done and won't do that much to make sure the change is secure after you're gone. You need to educate a wider circle in the organization with the expectation that the more people know what you have done and appreciate its importance, the less likely it will unravel when you are no longer around. Be sure to contact whoever you think has or should have some vested interest in seeing to it that the change becomes secure—staff, funders, overseers, customers, constituencies, media. They are the ones who can bring pressure to bear to make sure the change is not undone or misshaped. Your effort to enlarge the circle also provides you with important feedback as to where the change is still vulnerable and what actions should be taken that you might otherwise have ignored.

Who among all these interested players are the "custodians" you need? This leads to asking yourself more questions. Are their positions secure? Have I "dumped memory," telling them all I know about what has been done and what remains to be done? Do they know who continues to oppose the changes made and what to look out for from those quarters? Do they have the necessary resources (personnel, budgetary, etc.) that I think they need to secure the change? Do those in the wider circle know who the custodians are within the organization, and have lines of communication been established among them?

If you actually plan to leave the organization, all these questions have a greater sense of urgency. When others learn that you are moving on, it may alter the equation of just how secure the changes appear to be. If you can choose or influence the choice of your successor, take advantage of your leverage to educate her about the changes made—dumping memory, identifying potential allies and adversaries, and making clear how the change, if secured, can benefit her own agenda. Helping to obtain necessary personnel and budgetary resources before you leave can't help but impress her with the care you have taken to make the change work. If you make her job easier from the outset, it makes it easier for her to favorably entertain the changes that you think should be secured. With everyone else, spread the word in much the same way that your hypothetical leaving prompted widening the circle. If not your successor, who are the custodians you leave behind? Do they have the resources and lines of communication they need to carry on?

As noted in Chapter 2, when people get ready to move on, their exits are remembered as well as their entrances, and that goes for the legacies they leave behind, too. Do all you can to secure the change you worked so hard to put into place so that when you revisit that chapter of your career, you find a new status quo that is more to your liking, and someone tells you: "That's the way we do things around here." What prospector doesn't like happy endings as well as new beginnings?

NOTES

Introduction

1. *The Economist,* July 15, 2000, 64–65; Marion McGovern and Dennis Russell, *A New Brand of Expertise* (Oxford: Butterworth-Heinemann, 2001), p. 81.

2. "Loop," *Fast Company* (July 2001), 31.

3. Daniel Pink boldly asserts that "Most managers are toast." I wouldn't go that far. Free agents and the 75 percent of the workforce who do not operate independently still need higher-ups to help coordinate many of their undertakings, even as higher-ups make substantial adjustments of their own. Daniel Pink, *Free Agent Nation* (New York: Warner Books, 2001), p. 307.

4. *Merriam Webster's Collegiate Dictionary,* 10th ed. (Springfield, Mass.: Merriam-Webster, 1995), p. 315.

5. David W. Brown, *When Strangers Cooperate* (New York: The Free Press, 1995), p. 3.

Chapter 1

1. The work of Deal and Kennedy on "learning to read cultures" is useful here. See Terrence E. Deal and Allan A. Kennedy, *Corporate Cultures* (Reading, Mass.: Addison-Wesley Publishing Company, 1982), pp. 129–39. See also their more recent work, *The New Corporate Cultures* (Cambridge, Mass.: Perseus Publishing, 2000), pp. 1–18.

2. Edgar Schein, who has contributed so much to a richer understanding of what culture is, discusses the important assumptions that underlie behavior in a particular organization. See Edgar H. Schein, *Organizational Culture and Leadership,* 2nd ed. (San Francisco: Jossey-Bass, 1992), pp. 3–15.

3. Thomas Schelling was one of the first postwar economists to analyze coordination problems and how focal points help players find solutions. See *The Strategy of Conflict* (Cambridge, Mass.: Harvard University Press, 1960), pp. 55–57.

4. Amartya Sen, *Development as Freedom* (New York: Alfred A. Knopf, 1999), p. 273.

5. Aaron Wildavsky, *Budgeting: A Comparative Theory of Budgeting Processes* (New Brunswick, N.J.: Transaction Books, 1986), p. 322.

6. James March, *A Primer on Decision Making* (New York: The Free Press, 1994), p. 96.

7. *Merriam Webster's Collegiate Dictionary,* 10th ed. (Springfield, Mass.: Merriam-Webster, 1995), p. 866.

8. Jeffrey Pfeffer, *Managing with Power* (Cambridge, Mass.: Harvard Business School Press, 1992), pp. 66–68.

9. Dietrich Dörner, *The Logic of Failure* (New York: Metropolitan Books, 1996), p. 101.

Chapter 2

1. Daniel Klein, ed., *Reputation: Studies in the Voluntary Elicitation of Good Conduct* (Ann Arbor: University of Michigan Press, 1997), p. 32.

2. Robert Axelrod, *The Evolution of Cooperation* (New York: Basic Books, 1984), p. 110.

3. I first learned about the envelope game from J. Keith Murnighan, in *Bargaining Games* (New York: William Morrow and Company, 1992), pp. 191–94. It is a variant of a one-round, multiperson prisoner's dilemma game that, among other considerations, poses a conflict between individual and common gain.

4. My discussion here uses the concept of "commitment" developed by Thomas Schelling in *The Strategy of Conflict* (Cambridge, Mass.: Harvard University Press, 1960), pp. 21–46. Schelling argues that to establish the credibility of your offers, threats, etc. in a bargaining situation, sometimes you have to convince the other party that you are committed to your position by limiting your ability to change or abandon it.

Chapter 3

1. *Webster's Third New International Dictionary of the English Language* (Springfield, Mass.: G. & C. Merriam, 1964), p. 57.

2. When I ask students to go "bottom fishing" together in small classroom groups, each frames a problem arising in his or her workplace and offers it for discussion by the group. What often happens is that the group will put aside the frame offered and instead suggest new ways for their colleague to frame the problem. In the ensuing discussion, a more important or underlying problem may be identified, helping the student to reconsider just what the real problem is and how to proceed.

3. John J. Gabarro and John P. Kotter, "Managing Your Boss," *Harvard Business Review* (May–June 1993), 154.

4. Jeffrey Pfeffer, *New Directions for Organization Theory* (New York: Oxford University Press, 1997), pp. 116–20.

5. Such priorities were part of a Chivas Regal Report, "Working Americans: Emerging Values for the 1990's," summarized in *Understanding Organizations*, 4th ed., by Charles Handy (New York: Oxford University Press, 1993), p. 32.

6. The role play is based on a scenario originally developed by Robert House of Suffolk University in Boston, Mass.

Time Out: Storytelling in Organizations

1. James March, *A Primer on Decision Making* (New York: The Free Press, 1994), p. 199.

2. Herbert A. Simon, *The Sciences of the Artificial,* 2nd ed. (Cambridge, Mass.: MIT Press, 1981), pp. 63–65.

3. John Allen Paulos, *A Mathematician Reads the Newspaper* (New York: Anchor Books, 1996), p. 22.

4. David Lane, Franco Malerba, Robert Maxfield, and Luigi Orsenigo, "Choice and Action," Working Paper 95-01-004 (Santa Fe Institute, 1995), p. 27.

5. Robert D. Behn, "Management by Groping Along," *Journal of Policy Analysis and Management* 7, No. 4 (1988), 653–55.

Chapter 4

1. In medical circles, practitioners who please their customers but not their colleagues are considered "quacks."

2. Jerome Bruner, *The Process of Education* (Cambridge, Mass.: Harvard University Press, 1977), pp. 88–89.

3. This is in the spirit of what Peter Drucker said about "effective executives" more than thirty years ago. "The effective executive asks the specialist, 'What contribution from me do you require to make your contribution to the organization? When do you need this, how do you need it, and in what form?'" See Peter F. Drucker, *The Effective Executive* (New York: Harper & Row, 1966), p. 62.

4. Jacques Barzun, *Teacher in America* (Indianapolis, Ind.: Liberty Press, 1981), p. 386.

5. Some of my discussion here comes from work that I have done on professionalism. See "Professional Virtue," *Change* (November-December 1985), 8–9, 46–47; "Civic Virtue in America," *National Forum* (spring 1987), 39–41; and "Daring to be Unprofessional," *Higher Education Exchange* (1997), 10–13.

Chapter 5

1. John P. Kotter and Leonard A. Schlesinger, "Choosing Strategies for Change," *Harvard Business Review* (March–April 1979), Reprint 79202, pp. 5–6.

2. This example comes from Charles E. Lindblom and David K. Cohen, *Usable Knowledge* (New Haven: Yale University Press, 1979), p. 19. "For the [social] learning we have in mind in such cases comes from actual experience that upsets old attitudes and dispositions" (p. 18).

3. I draw here on my work in *When Strangers Cooperate* (New York: The Free Press, 1995), p. 32: "Enough others is a simple way to express what is not so simple a proposition—the idea of critical mass. Critical mass is a threshold. It does not relate to sheer numbers of people, but to how many are needed to make coordination successful. . . . In any particular social context, there is no predetermined number of people who constitute a critical mass. It all depends."

4. Ibid., p. 123. In another context, William James said, "faith in a fact can help create the fact." William James, *The Will to Believe* (New York: Dover, 1956), p. 25.

5. Ibid., pp. 76–79.

6. Ibid., p. 36.

7. Ibid., p. 128: "When we seek to change and improve a situation, there is always the possibility that we won't—not because of a failure to get others' cooperation, but because that cooperation leads to problems that we did not foresee."

INDEX

ABOUT THE AUTHOR

David W. Brown is currently professor of professional practice at the Milano Graduate School of Management and Urban Policy of New School University in New York City. Before that he taught for ten years at the Yale School of Management. He is the author of *When Strangers Cooperate*, numerous articles, and teaching cases, and is coeditor of the *Higher Education Exchange*, a publication of the Kettering Foundation.

His organizational experience includes for profit firms, nonprofit corporations, public authorities, and governmental agencies, where he has been a law partner, board member, state commissioner, deputy mayor, and college president.

Brown holds a B.A. in English from Princeton University and a J.D. from Harvard Law School.

He lives in New York City with his wife, Alice, and tries to skate five miles every day in Central Park.